The Art of Poetry volume 9

Edexcel poetry: Relationships

Published by Peripeteia Press Ltd.

First published March 2017

ISBN: 978-0-9954671-5-6

Peripeteia.webs.com

Contents

With thanks to Carol Atherton, Johanna Harrison and Neil Jones. And to my family for letting me hide away and keep writing.

General Introduction to the The Art of Poetry series

The philosopher Nietzsche described his work as 'the greatest gift that [mankind] has ever been given'. The Elizabethan poet Edmund Spenser hoped his book *The Faerie Queene* would magically transform its readers into noblemen. In comparison, our aims for *The Art of Poetry* series of books are a little more modest. Fundamentally we aim to provide books that will be of maximum use to English students and their teachers. In our experience, few students read essays on poems, yet, whatever specification they are studying, they have to write analytical essays on poetry. So, we've offering some models, written in a lively and accessible style. We believe too that the essay as a form needs championing, especially when so many revision books for students present information in broken down note form.

For Volume 1 we chose canonical poems for several reasons: Firstly, they are simply great poems, well worth reading and studying; secondly, we chose poems from across time so that they sketch in outline major developments in English poetry, from the Elizabethan period up until the present day, so that the volume works as an introduction to poetry and poetry criticism. And, being canonical poems, this selection often crops up on GCSE and A-level specifications, so our material will be useful critical accompaniment and revision material. Our popular volumes 2-5 focused on poems set at A-level by the Edexcel and AQA boards respectively. In this current volume, we turn our focus back to GCSE, providing critical support for students reading poems about relationships from Edexcel's poetry anthology. In particular, we hope to inspire those students aiming to reach the very highest grades.

Introduction to Volume 9: Relationships

An adventure into what one apprehends

When writing about themes, students often simply state what they think the major theme of a poem to be. As Edexcel has kindly arranged these poems as a thematic cluster, writing something like 'this is a poem about love and relationships' doesn't get us very far. Sometimes readers also labour under a misconception about the nature of poetry, believing that poems have secret messages that poets annoyingly have hidden under deliberately obscure language. The task of the reader becomes to decode the obscure language and extract this buried message. Unsurprisingly, this misconception of poetry as a sort of fancy subcategory of fables makes readers wonder why poets went to all the irritating trouble of hiding their messages in the first place. If they had something to say, why didn't the poet just say it and save everyone a lot of unnecessary fuss and bother? Why couldn't Browning, for instance, have just said that rich, powerful men can be abusive monsters?

The Romantic poet, John Keats's comment about distrusting poetry that has a 'palpable design' on the reader has been much quoted. For Keats, and many poets, a 'palpable design' is an aspect of rhetoric and particularly of propaganda and a poem is not just a piece of propaganda for a poet's ideas. As the modern poet, George Szirtes puts it, poems are not 'rhymed advertisements for the already formed views of poets'. Here's George discussing the issue: 'A proper poem has to be a surprise: no surprise for the poet no surprise for the reader, said Robert Frost and I think that he and Keats were essentially right. A proper poem should arise out of a naked unguarded experience that elicits surprise in the imagination by extending the consciousness in some way. Poetry is not what one knows but an adventure into what one apprehends.'[1]

Most poems are not merely prettified presentations of a poet's preformed views about a particular theme or issue; they are more like thought experiments or journeys of exploration and discovery. In other words, poetry, like all art, is equipment for thinking and feeling. So, instead of writing that 'poem x is about love and relationships' try to think more carefully through what is interesting or unusual or surprising about the poem's exploration of these subjects. Sometimes the nature of the love or the central relationship will be obvious, as in poems exploring romantic love; at other times the type of love might be more unusual or crop up in an incongruous context. Approach a poem with questions in mind: What does the poem have to say about its theme? What angle does the poet take; is the poem celebratory, mournful, exploratory? To what extent does the poem take up arms and argue for something and have a 'palpable design'? Is their attitude to the subject consistent or does it change? To what extent is the poem philosophical or emotional? Do we learn something new, does it change how we think or feel? How might the poem have extended our thinking about its subject?

It would be trite to conclude that all these various poems are merely telling us that love is a wonderful thing and that good relationships are central to a fulfilling life. Love spurned, after all, can curdle into hate. Love for one person, nation or idea can lead to antipathy towards other people, nations or ideas. Are there any poems in Edexcel's anthology criticising relationships? Are there any instances of destructive, jealous or unhealthy relationships in these poems? Of course there are. Are there any unusual or counterintuitive

---

[1] http://georgeszirtes.blogspot.co.uk/

manifestations of love and relationships? The madness of love? The selfishness or possessiveness of love? Relationships as constraining and oppressive? Is the love between two lovers or does the poem depict platonic or familial love? Is the poem a meditation on the nature of love or a powerful expression of the experience of being in love? We're sure you get the idea. A key thing to remember is that 'love' is both a feeling and an idea. And ideas of love change over time and space. An adventure into what you apprehend is a great way to conceptualise a poem. And it's very productive too as a way to think about writing poetry criticism.

How to analyse a poem (seen or unseen)

A list of ingredients, not a recipe

Firstly, what not to do: sometimes pupils have been so programmed to spot poetic features such as alliteration that they start analysis of a poem with close reading of these micro aspects of technique. This is never a good idea. A far better strategy is to begin by trying to develop an overall understanding of what you think the poem is about. While, obvioiusly, all theses poems are about relationships, the nature of these relationships vary widely what they have say about this topic is also highly varried. Once you've established the central concerns, you can delve into the poem's interior, examining its inner workings in the light of these. And you should be flexible enough to adapt, refine or even reject your initial thoughts in the light of your investigation. The essential thing is to make sure that whether you're discussing imagery or stanza form, sonic effects or syntax, enjambment or vocabulary, you always explore the significance of the feature in terms of meanings and effect.

Someone once compared texts to cakes. When you're presented with a cake the first thing you notice is what it looks like. Probably the next thing you'll do is taste it and find out if you like the flavour. This aesthetic experience will come first. Only later might you investigate the ingredients and how it was made. Adopting a uniform reading strategy is like a recipe; it sets out what you must, do step by step, in a predetermined order. This can be helpful, especially when you start reading and analysing poems. Hence in our first volume in The Art of Poetry series we explored each poem under the same subheadings of narrator, characters, imagery, patterns of sound, form & structure and contexts, and all our essays followed essentially the same direction. Of course, this is a reasonable strategy for reading poetry and will stand you in good stead. However, this present volume takes a different, more flexible approach, because this book is designed for students aiming for levels 7 to 9, or A to A* in old currency, and to reach the highest levels your work needs to be a bit more conceptual, critical and individual. Writing frames are useful for beginners, like stabilisers when you learn to ride a bike. But, if you wish to write top level essays you need to develop your own frames.

Read our essays and you'll find that they all include the same principle ingredients – detailed, 'fine-grained' reading of crucial elements of poetry, imagery, form, rhyme and so forth - but each essay starts in a different way and each one has a slightly different focus or weight of attention on the various aspects that make up a poem. Once you feel you have mastered the apprentice strategy of reading all poems in the same way, we strongly recommend you put this generic essay recipe approach to one side and move on to a new way of reading, an approach that can change depending on the nature of the poem you're reading.

Follow your nose

Having established what you think a poem is about - its theme and what is interesting about the poet's treatment of the theme (the conceptual bit) - rather than then working through a pre-set agenda, decide what you honestly think are the most interesting aspects of the poem and start analysing these closely. This way your response will be original and you'll be writing about material you find most interesting. In other words, you're foregrounding yourself as an individual, critical reader. These most interesting aspects might be ideas or technique based, or both.

Follow your own, informed instincts, trust in your own critical intelligence as a reader. If you're writing about material that genuinely interests you, your writing is likely to be interesting for the examiner too. And, obviously, take advice to from your teacher too, use their expertise.

Because of the focus on sonic effects and imagery other aspects of poems are often overlooked by students. It is a rare student, for instance, who notices how punctuation works in a poem and who can write about it convincingly. Few students write about the contribution of the unshowy function words, such as pronouns, prepositions or conjunctions, yet these words are crucial to any text. Of course, it would be a highly risky strategy to focus your whole essay on a seemingly innocuous and incidental detail of a poem. But noticing what others do not and coming at things from an unusual angle are as important to writing great essays as they are to the production of great poetry.

So, in summary, when reading a poem have a check list in mind, but don't feel you must follow someone else's generic essay recipe. Don't feel that you must always start with a consideration of imagery if the poem you're analysing has, for instance, an eye-catching form. Consider the significance of major features, such as imagery, vocabulary, sonic patterns and form. Try to write about these aspects in terms of their contribution to themes and effects. But also follow your nose, find your own direction, seek out aspects that genuinely engage you and write about these. Try to develop your own essay style.

The essays in this volume provide examples and we hope they will encourage you to go your own way, at least to some extent, and to make discoveries for yourself. No single essay could possibly cover everything that could be said about any one of these poems; aiming to create comprehensive essays like this would be utterly foolish. And we have not tried to do so. Nor are our essays meant to be models for exam essays – they're far too long for that. They do, however, illustrate the sort of conceptualised, critical and 'fine-grained' exploration demanded for top grades at GCSE and beyond. There's always more to be discovered, more to say, space in other words for you to develop some original reading of your own, space for you to write your own individual essay recipe.

Writing literature essays

The Big picture and the small

An essay itself can be a form of art. And writing a great essay takes time, skill and practice. And also expert advice. Study the two figures in the picture carefully and describe what you can see. Channel your inner Sherlock Holmes to add any deductions you are able to form about the image. Before reading what we have to say, write your description out as a prose paragraph. Probably you'll have written something along the following lines:

First off, the overall impression: this picture is very blurry. Probably this indicates that either this is a very poor quality reproduction, or that it is a copy of a very small detail from a much bigger image that has been magnified several times. The image shows a stocky man and a medium-sized dog, both orientated towards something to their left, which suggests there is some point of interest in that direction. From the man's rustic dress (smock, breeches, clog-like boots) the picture is either an old one or a modern one depicting the past. The man appears to be carrying a stick and there's maybe a bag on his back. From all of these details we can probably deduce that he's a peasant, maybe a farmer or a shepherd.

Now do the same thing for picture two. We have even less detail here and again the picture's blurry. Particularly without the benefit of colour it's hard to determine what we're seeing other than a horizon and maybe the sky. We might just be able to make out that in the centre of the picture is the shape of the sun. From the reflection, we can deduce that the image is of the sun either setting or rising over water. If it is dawn this usually symbolises hope, birth and new beginnings; if the sun is setting it conventionally symbolises the opposite – the end of things, the coming of night/ darkness, death.

If you're a sophisticated reader, you might well start to think about links between the two images. Are they, perhaps, both details from the same single larger image, for instance.

Well, this image might be even harder to work out. Now we don't even have

a whole figure, just a leg, maybe, sticking up in the air. Whatever is happening here, it looks painful and we can't even see the top half of the body. From the upside orientation, we might guess that the figure is or has fallen. If we put this image with the one above, we might think the figure has fallen into water as there are horizontal marks on the image that could be splashes. From the quality of this image we can deduce that this is an even smaller detail blown-up.

You may be wondering by now why we've suddenly moved into rudimentary art appreciation. On the other hand, you may already have worked out the point of this exercise. Either way, bear with us, because this is the last picture for you to describe and analyse. So, what have we here?

Looks like another peasant, again from the past, perhaps medieval (?) from the smock-like dress, clog-like shoes and the britches. This character is also probably male and seems to be pushing some wooden apparatus from left to right. From the ridges at the bottom left of the image we can surmise that he's working the land, probably driving a plough. Noticeably the figure has his back to us; we see his turned away from us, suggesting his whole concentration is on the task at hand. In the background appear to be sheep, which would fit with our impression that this is an image of farming. It seems likely that this image and the first one come from the same painting. They have a similar style and subject and it is possible that these sheep belong to our first character. This image is far less blurry than the other one. Either it is a better-quality reproduction, or this is a larger, more significant detail extracted from the original source. If this is a significant detail it's interesting that we cannot see the character's face. From this we can deduce that he's not important in and of himself; rather he's a representative figure and the important thing is what he is and what he isn't looking at.

Okay, we hope we haven't stretched your patience too far. What's the point of all this? Well, let's imagine we prefixed the paragraphs above with an introduction, along the following lines: 'The painter makes this picture interesting and powerful by using several key techniques and details' and that we added a conclusion, along the lines of 'So now I have shown how the painter has made this picture interesting and powerful through the use of a number of key techniques and details'. Finally, substitute painter and picture for writer and text. If we put together our paragraphs into an essay what would be its strengths and weaknesses? What might be a better way of writing our essay?

Consider the strengths first off. The best bits of our essay, we humbly suggest, are the bits where we begin to explain what we are seeing, when we do the Holmes like deductive thinking. Another strength might be that we have started to make links between the various images, or parts of a larger image, to see how they work together to provide us more information. A corresponding weakness is that each of our paragraphs seems like a separate chunk of writing. The weaker parts of the paragraphs are where we simply describe what we can see. More importantly though, if we used our comments on image one as our first paragraph we seem to have started in a rather random way. Why should we have begun our essay with that image? What was the logic behind that? And most importantly of all, if this image is an analogue for a specific aspect of a text, such as a poem's imagery or a novel's dialogue we have dived straight into to analysing this technical aspect before we're established any overall sense of the painting/ text. And this is a very common fault with GCSE English Literature essays. As we've said before and will keep saying, pupils start writing detailed micro-analysis of a detail such as alliteration before they have established the big picture of what the text is about and what the answer to the question they've been set might be. Without this big picture it's very difficult to write about the significance of the micro details. And the major marks for English essays are reserved for explanations of the significance and effects generated by a writer's craft.

Now we'll try a different and much better approach. Let's start off with the big picture, the whole image. The painting on the next page is called *Landscape with the fall of Icarus*. It's usually attributed to the Renaissance artist, Pieter Breughel and was probably painted in the 1560s. Icarus is a character from Greek mythology. He was the son of the brilliant inventor, Daedalus. Trapped on Crete by the evil King Minos, Daedalus and Icarus managed to escape when the inventor created pairs of giant feathered wings. Before they took to sky Daedalus warned his son not to get too excited and fly too near the sun as the wings were held together by wax that might melt. Icarus didn't listen, however. The eventual result was that he plummeted back to earth, into the sea more precisely and was killed.

Applying this contextual knowledge to the painting we can see that the image is about how marginal Icarus' tragedy is in the big picture. Conventionally we'd expect any image depicting such a famous myth to make Icarus's fall the dramatic centre of attention. The main objects of this painting, however, are emphatically not the falling boy hitting the water. Instead our eye is drawn to the peasant in the centre of the painting, pushing his plough (even more so in colour as his shirt is the only red object in an otherwise greeny-yellow landscape) and the stately galleon sailing calmly past those protruding legs. Seeing the whole image, we can appreciate the significance of the shepherd and the ploughman looking up and down and to the left. The point being made is how they don't even notice the tragedy because they have work to do and need to get on with their lives. The animals too seem unconcerned. As W. H. Auden's puts it, in lines from *Musée des Beaux Arts*, 'everything turns away / Quite leisurely from the disaster'.

To sum up, when writing an essay on any literary text do not begin with close-up analysis of micro-details. Begin instead with establishing the whole picture: What the text is about, what key techniques the writer uses, when it was written, what sort of text it is, what effects it has on the reader. Then, when you zoom in to examine smaller details, such as imagery, individual words, metre or sonic techniques you can discuss these in relation to their significance in terms of this bigger picture.

What would our art appreciation essay look like now?

Paragraph #1: Introduction – myth of Icarus, date of painting, the way our eyes is drawn away from his tragic death to much more ordinary life going around him. Significance of this – even tragic suffering goes on around us without us even noticing, we're too busy getting on with our lives.

Paragraph #2: We could, of course, start with our first figure and follow the same order as we've presented the images here. But wouldn't it make more logical sense to discuss first the biggest, more prominent images in the painting first? So, our first paragraph is about the ploughman and his horse.

How his figure placed centrally and is bent downwards towards the ground and turned left away from us etc.

Paragraph #3: The next most prominent image is the ship. Also moving from right to left, as if the main point of interest in the painting is off in that direction. Here we could consider the other human agricultural figure, the shepherd and his dog and, of course, the equally oblivious sheep.

Paragraph #4: Having moved on to examining background details in the painting we could discuss the symbolism of the sun on the horizon. While this could be the sun rising, the context of the story suggests it is more likely to be setting. The pun of the sun/son going down makes sense.

Paragraph #5: Finally, we can turn our attention to the major historical and literary figure in this painting, Icarus and how he is presented. This is the key image in terms of understanding the painting's purpose and effect.

Paragraph #6: Conclusion. What is surprising about this picture. How do the choices the painter makes affect us as viewer/ reader? Does this painting make Icarus's story seem more pathetic, more tragic or something else?

Now, all you have to do is switch from a painting to a poem.

Big pictures, big cakes, recipes and lists of instructions; following your own nose and going your own way. Whatever metaphors we use, your task is to bring something personal and individual to your critical reading of poems and to your essay writing.

Writing comparative essays

The following is adapted from our discussion of this topic in *The Art of Writing English Literature Essays* A-level course companion, and is a briefer version, tailored to the GCSE exam task. Fundamentally comparative essays want you to display not only your ability to intelligently talk about literary texts, but also your ability to make meaningful connections between them. The first starting point is your topic. This must be broad enough to allow substantial thematic overlapping of the texts. However, too little overlap and it will be difficult to connect the texts; too much overlap and your discussion will be lopsided and one-dimensional. In the case of the GCSE exam, the broad topic will, of course, be relationships. The exam question will ask you to focus on the methods used by the poets to explore how two poems present this theme. You will also be directed to write specifically on language and imagery [AO2] as well as on the contexts in which the poems were written [AO3].

One poem from the anthology will be specified and printed on the paper. You will then have to choose a companion poem. Selecting the right poem for interesting comparison is obviously very important. Obviously, you should prepare for this task beforehand by pairing up the poems, especially as you will only have about 35 minutes to complete this task. You will also be asked to compare unseen poems, so grasping how best to write comparative essays is essential to your chance of reaching the top grades. To think about this task visually, you don't want Option A, below, [not enough overlap] or Option B [two much overlap]. You want Option C. This option allows substantial common links to be built between your chosen texts where discussion arises from both fundamental similarities AND differences.

20

Option A: too many differences

Option B: too many similarities

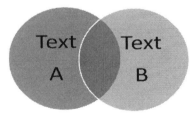

Option C: suitable number of similarities and differences

The final option will generate the most interesting discussion as it will allow substantial similarities to emerge as well as differences. The best comparative essays actually find that what seemed like clear similarities become subtle differences and vice versa while still managing to find rock solid similarities to build their foundations on.

Check the mark scheme for this question and you'll notice that to reach the top grade your comparison must be 'well-structured'. How should you structure a comparative essay? Consider the following alternatives. Which one is best and why?

Essay Structure #1

1. Introduction
2. Main body paragraph #1 - Text A
3. Main body paragraph #2 - Text A
4. Main body paragraph #3 - Text B
5. Main body paragraph #4 - Text B
6. Conclusion

Essay Structure #2

1. Introduction
2. Main body paragraph #1 - Text A
3. Main body paragraph #2 - Text A
4. Main body paragraph #3 - Text B
5. Main body paragraph #4 - Text B
6. Comparison of main body paragraphs #1 & #3 - Text A + B
7. Comparison of main body paragraphs #2 & #4 - Text A + B
8. Conclusion

Essay Structure #3

1. Introduction
2. Main body paragraph #1 - Text A + B
3. Main body paragraph #2 - Text A + B
4. Main body paragraph #3 - Text A + B

5. Main body paragraph #4 - Text A+ B

6. Conclusion

We hope you will agree that 3 is the optimum option. Option 1 is the dreaded 'here is everything I know about text A, followed by everything I know by Text B' approach where the examiner has to work out what the connections are between the texts. This will score the lowest marks. Option 2 is better: There is some attempt to compare the two texts. However, it is a very inefficient way of comparing the two texts. For comparative essay writing the most important thing is to discuss both texts together. This is the most effective and efficient way of achieving your overall aim. Option 3 does this by comparing and contrasting the two texts under common umbrella headings. This naturally encourages comparison. Using comparative discourse markers, such as 'similarly', 'in contrast to', 'conversely' 'likewise' and 'however' also facilitates effective comparison.

When writing about each poem, make sure you do not work chronologically through a poem, summarising the content of each stanza. Responses of this sort typically start with 'In the first stanza' and employ discourse markers of time rather than comparison, such as 'after', 'next', 'then' and so forth. Even if your reading is analytical rather than summative, your essay should not work through the poem from the opening to the ending. Instead, make sure you write about the ideas explored in both texts (themes), the feelings and effects generated and the techniques the poets utilise to achieve these.

Writing about language

Poems are paintings as well as windows; we look at them as well as through them. As you know, special attention should be paid to language in poetry because of all the literary art forms poetry, in particular, employs language in a precise, self-conscious and distinctive way. Ideally in poetry, every word should count. Analysis of language falls into distinct categories:

- By diction we mean the vocabulary used in a poem. A poem might be composed from the ordinary language of everyday speech or it might use elaborate, technical or elevated phrasing. Or both. At one time, some words and types of words were considered inappropriate for the rarefied field of poetry. The great Irish poet, W. B. Yeats never referred to modern technology in his poetry, there are no cars, or tractors or telephones, because he did not consider such things fitting for poetry. When much later, Philip Larkin used swear words in his otherwise well-mannered verse the effect was deeply shocking. Modern poets have pretty much dispensed with the idea of there being an elevated literary language appropriate for poetry. Hence in the Edexcel anthology you'll find all sorts of modern, everyday language.

- Grammatically a poem may use complex or simple sentences [the key to which is the conjunctions]; it might employ a wash of adjectives and adverbs, or it may rely extensively on the bare force of nouns and verbs. Picking out and exploring words from specific grammatical classes has the merit of being both incisive and usually illuminating.

- Poets might mix together different types, conventions and registers of language, moving, for example, between formal and informal, spoken and written, modern and archaic, and so forth. Arranging the diction in the poem in terms of lexico-semantic fields, by register or by etymology, helps reveal underlying patterns of meaning.

- For almost all poems imagery is a crucial aspect of language. Broadly imagery is a synonym for description and can be broken down into two types, sensory and figurative. Sensory imagery means the words and phrases that appeal to our senses, to touch and taste, hearing, smell and sight. Sensory imagery is evocative; it helps to take us into the world of the poem to share the experience being described. Figurative imagery, in particular, is always significant. As we have mentioned, not all poems rely on metaphors and similes; these devices are only part of a poet's box of tricks, but figurative language is always important when it occurs because it compresses multiple meanings into itself. To use a technical term figurative images are polysemic - they contain many meanings. Try writing out the all the meanings contained in a metaphor in a more concise and economical way. Even simple, everyday metaphors compress meaning. If we want to say our teacher is fierce and powerful and that we fear his or her wrath, we can more concisely say our teacher is a dragon.

Writing about patterns of sound

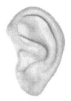 Like painters, some poets have powerful visual imaginations, while other poets have stronger auditory imaginations are more like musicians. And some poems are like paintings, others are more like pieces of music.

Firstly, what not to do: Tempting as it may be to spot sonic features of a poem and list these, don't do this. Avoid something along the lines of 'The poet uses alliteration here and the rhyme scheme is ABABCDCDEFEFGG'. Sometimes, indeed, it may be tempting to set out the poem's whole rhyme scheme like this. Resist the temptation: This sort of identification of features is worth zero marks. Marks in exams are reserved for attempts to link techniques to meanings and to effects.

Probably many of us have been sitting in English lessons listening somewhat sceptically as our English teacher explains the surprisingly specific significance of a seemingly random piece of alliteration in a poem. Something along the lines 'The double d sounds here reinforce a sense of invincible strength' or 'the harsh repetition of the 't' sounds suggests anger'. Through all our minds at some point may have passed the idea that, in these instances, English teachers appear to be using some sort of Enigma-style secret symbolic decoding machine that reveals how particular patterns of sounds have such definite encoded meanings.

And this sort of thing is not all nonsense. Originally deriving from an oral tradition, poems are, of course, written for the ear as much as for the eye, to be heard as much as read. A poem is a soundscape as much as it is a set of meanings. Sounds are, however, difficult to tie to very definite meanings and effects. By way of example, the old BBC Radiophonic workshop, which produced ambient sounds for radio and television programmes, used the same sounds in different contexts, knowing that the audience would perceive them in the appropriate way because of that context. Hence the sound of bacon sizzling, of an audience clapping and of feet walking over gravel were actually recordings of an identical sound. Listeners heard them differently because of the context. So, we may, indeed, be able to spot the repeated 's' sounds in a poem, but whether this creates a hissing sound, yes like a snake, or the susurration of the sea will depend on the context within the poem and the ears of the reader. Whether a sound is soft and soothing or harsh and grating is also open to interpretation.

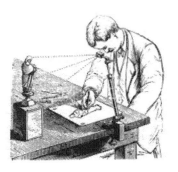

The idea of connecting these sounds to meanings or significance is a productive one. And your analysis will be most convincing if you use several pieces of evidence together. In other words, rather than try to pick out individual examples of sonic effects we recommend you explore the weave or pattern of sounds, the effects these generate and their contribution to feelings and ideas. For example, this might mean examining how alliteration and assonance are used together to achieve a particular mimetic effect.

Writing about form & structure

As you know, there are no marks for simply identifying textual features. This holds true for language, sounds and also for form. Consider instead the relationship between a poem's form and its content, themes and effects. Form is not merely decorative or ornamental: A poem's meanings and effects are generated through the interplay of form and content. Broadly speaking the form can either work with or against a poem's content. Conventionally a sonnet, for instance, is about love, whereas a limerick is a comic form. A serious love poem in the form of a limerick would be unusual, as would a sonnet about an old man with a beard.

Sometimes poetic form can create an ironic backdrop to highlight an aspect of content. An example would be a formally elegant poem about something  monstrous. Browning's *My Last Duchess* springs to mind. The artist Grayson Perry uses form in this ironic way. Rather than depicting the sort of picturesque, idealised images we expect of ceramics, Perry's pots and urns depict modern life in bright, garish colours. The urn pictured, for instance, is entitled *Modern Family* and depicts two gay men with a boy who they have presumably adopted. A thrash metal concert inside a church, a philosophical essay via text message, a fine crystal goblet filled with cherryade would be further examples of ironic relationships between message and medium, content and context or form.

****

Reading form

Put a poem before your eyes. Start off taking a panoramic perspective: Think of the forest, not the trees. Perhaps mist over your eyes a bit. Don't even read the words, just look at the poem, like at a painting. Is the poem slight, thin, fat, long, short? What is the relation of whiteness to blackness? Why might the poet have chosen this shape? Does it look regular or irregular? A poem about a long winding river will probably look rather different from one about a small pebble, or should do. Unless form is being employed ironically. Now read the poem a couple of times. First time, fast as you can, second time more slowly and carefully. How does the visual layout of the poem relate to what it seems to be about? Does this form support, or create a tension against, the content? Is the form one you recognise, like a sonnet, or is it more open, more irregular like free verse? Usually the latter is obvious from the irregularity of the stanzas, line lengths and lack of metre or rhyme.

As Hurley and O'Neill explain in *Poetic Form: An Introduction*, like genre, form sets expectations: 'In choosing form, poets bring into play associations and expectations which they may then satisfy, modify or subvert'.[2] We've already suggested that if we see a poem is a sonnet or a limerick this recognition will set up expectations about the nature of the poem's content. The same thing works on a smaller level; once we have noticed that a poem's first stanza is a quatrain, we expect it to continue in this neat, orderly fashion. If the quatrain's rhyme scheme is xaxa, xbxb, in which only the second and fourth lines rhyme, we reasonably expect that the next stanza will be xcxc. So, if it isn't we need to consider why.

After taking in the big picture in terms of choice of form in relation to content

---

[2] Hurley & O'Neill, *Poetic Form, An Introduction*, p.3

zoom in: Explore the stanza form, lineation, punctuation, the use of enjambment and caesura. Single line stanzas draw attention to themselves. If they are end-stopped they can suggest isolation, separation. Couplets imply twoness. Stanzas of three lines are called tercets and feature in villanelles and terza rima. On the page, both these forms tend to look rather delicate, especially if separated from each other by the silence of white space. Often balanced through rhyme, quatrains look a bit more robust and sturdy. Cinquains are swollen quatrains in which the last line often seems to throw the stanza out of balance.

Focus in on specific examples and on points of transition. For instance, if a poem has four regular quatrains followed by a couplet, examine the effect of this change. If we've been ticking along nicely in iambic metre and suddenly trip on a trochee, examine why. Consider regularity. Closed forms of poems, such as sonnets, are highly regular with set rhyme schemes, metre and number of lines. The opposite form is called 'open', the most extreme version of which is free verse. In free verse poems, the poet dispenses with any set metre, rhyme scheme or recognisable traditional form. What stops this sort of poetry from being prose chopped up to look like verse? The care of the design on the page. Hence, we need to focus here on lineation. Enjambment runs over lines and makes connections; caesura pauses a line and separates words. Lots of enjambment generates a sense of the language running away from the speaker. Lots of caesuras generate a halting, hesitant, choppy movement to lines. Opposites, these devices work in tandem and where they fall is always significant in a good poem.

Remember poetic form is never merely decorative. And bear in mind too the fact that the most volatile materials require the strongest containers.

Nice to metre...
A brief guide to metre and rhythm in poetry

Why express yourself in poetry? Why read words dressed up and expressed as a poem? What can you get from poetry that you can't from prose? There are many compelling answers to these questions. Here, though, we're going to concentrate on one aspect of the unique appeal of poetry – the structure of sound in poetry. Whatever our stage of education, we are all already sophisticated at detecting and using structured sound. Try reading the  following sentences without any variation whatsoever in how each sound is emphasised, and they will quickly lose what essential human characteristics they have. The sentences will sound robotic. So, in a sense, we won't be teaching anything new here. It's just that in poetry the structure of sound is carefully unusually crafted and created. It becomes a key part of what a poem is.

We will introduce a few new key technical terms along the way, but the ideas are straightforward. Individual sounds [syllables] are either stressed [emphasised, sounding louder and longer] or unstressed. As well as clustering into words and sentences for meaning, these sounds [syllables] cluster into rhythmic groups or feet, producing the poem's metre, which is the characteristic way its rhythm works.

In some poems, the rhythm is very regular and may even have a name, such as iambic pentameter. At the other extreme a poem may have no discernible regularity at all. As we have said, this is called free verse. It is vital to remember that the sound in a good poem is structured so that it combines effectively with the meanings.

For example, take a look at these two lines from Marvell's *To his Coy Mistress*:

'But at my back I alwaies hear
Times winged Chariot hurrying near:'

Forgetting the rhythms for a moment, Marvell is basically saying at this point 'Life is short, Time flies, and it's after us'. Now concentrate on the rhythm of his words.

- In the first line every other syllable is stressed: 'at', 'back', 'al', 'hear'.
- Each syllable before these is unstressed 'But', 'my', 'I', 'aies'.
- This is a regular beat or rhythm which we could write
  ti TUM / ti TUM / ti TUM / ti TUM , with the / separating the feet. ['Feet' is the technical term for metrical units of sound]
- This type of two beat metrical pattern is called iambic, and because there are four feet in the line, it is tetrameter. So this line is in 'iambic tetrameter'. [Tetra is Greek for four]
- Notice that 'my' and 'I' being unstressed diminishes the speaker, and we are already prepared for what is at his 'back', what he can 'hear' to be bigger than him, since these sounds are stressed.

- On the next line, the iambic rhythm is immediately broken off, since the next line hits us with two consecutive stressed syllables straight off: 'Times' 'wing'. Because a pattern had been established, when it suddenly changes the reader feels it, the words feel crammed together more urgently, the beats of the rhythm are closer, some little parcels of time have gone missing.

A physical rhythmic sensation is created of time slipping away, running out. This subtle sensation is enhanced by the stress-unstress-unstress pattern of words that follow, 'chariot hurrying' [TUM-ti-ti, TUM-ti-ti]. So the hurrying sounds underscore the meaning of the words.

14 ways of looking at a poem

Though conceived as pre-reading exercises, most of these tasks work just as well for revision.

1. Mash them (1) – mix together lines from two or more poems. The students' task is to untangle the poems from each other.

2. Mash them (2) – the second time round make the task significantly harder. Rather than just mixing whole lines, mash the poems together more thoroughly, words, phrases, images and all, so that unmashing seems impossible. At first sight.

3. Dock the last stanza or few lines from a poem. The students should come up with their own endings for the poem. Compare with the poet's version. Or present the poem without its title. Can the students come up with a suitable one?

4. Break a poem into segments. Split the class into groups. Each group work in isolation on their segment and feedback on what they discover. Then their task is to fit the poem and their ideas about it together as a whole.

5. Give the class the first and last stanza of a poem. Their task is to provide the filling. They can choose to attempt the task at beginner level (in prose) or at world class level (in poetry).

6. Add superfluous words to a poem. Start off with obvious interventions, such as the interjection of blatantly alien, noticeable words. Try smuggling 'pineapple', 'bourbon' and 'haberdashers' into any of the poems and see if you can get it past the critical sensors.

7. Repeat the exercise – This time using much less extravagant words. Try to smuggle in a few intensifiers, such as 'really', 'very' and 'so'. Or extra adjectives.

8. Collapse the lineation in a poem and present it as continuous prose. The students' task is to put it back into verse. Discussing the various pros and cons or various possible arrangements – short lines, long lines, irregular lines - can be very productive. Pay particular attention to line breaks and the words that end them. After a whatever-time-you- deem-fit, give the class the pattern of the first stanza. They then have to decide how to arrange the next stanza. Drip feed the rest of the poem to them.

9. Find a way to present the shapes of each poem on the page without the words. The class should work through each poem, two minutes at a time, speculating on what the shape might tell us about the content of the poem. This exercise works especially well as a starter activity. We recommend you use two poems at a time, as the comparison helps students to recognise and appreciate different shapes.

10. Test the thesis that an astute reader can recognise poems by men from those written by women. Give the class one of the poems such as *Sonnet 43* without the name of the poet. Ask them to identify

whether the writer is male or female and to explain their reasons for identifying them as such.

11. Split the class into groups. Each group should focus their analysis on a different feature of the poem. Start with the less obvious aspects: Group 1 should concentrate on enjambment and caesuras; group 2 on punctuation; group 3 on the metre and rhythm; group 4 on function words – conjunctions, articles, prepositions. 2-5 mins. only. Then swap focus, four times. Share findings.

12. In *Observations on Poetry*, Robert Graves wrote that 'rhymes properly used are the good servants whose presence at the dinner-table gives the guests a sense of opulent security; never awkward or over-clever, they hand the dishes silently and professionally. You can trust them not to interrupt the conversation or allow their personal disagreements to come to the notice of the guests; but some of them are getting very old for their work'. Explore the poets' use of rhyme in the light of Graves' comment. Are the rhymes ostentatiously original or old hat? Do they stick out of the poem or are they neatly tucked in? Are they dutiful servants of meaning or noisy disrupters of the peace?

13. The Romantic poet, John Keats, claimed that 'we hate poetry that has a palpable design upon us – and if we do not agree seems to put its hand its breeches pock'. Apply his comment to this selection of poems. Do any seem to have a 'palpable design' on the reader? If so, how does the poem want us to respond?

14. Each student should crunch the poem down to one word per line. Discuss this process as a class. Project the poem so the whole class can see it and start the crunching process by indicating and then crossing-out the function words from each line. Now discuss which of the remaining words is most important. This will also give you an opportunity to refer to grammatical terms, such as nouns and verbs. Once each line has been reduced to one word, from this list, pupils should crunch again. This time all that should remain are the five most important words in the whole poem. Now they need to write two or three sentences for each of these words explaining exactly why they are so important and why the poet didn't choose any of the possible synonyms.

'Poetry is only there to frame the silence. There is silence between each verse and silence at the end.'

ALICE OSWALD

John Keats, *La Belle Dame sans Merci*

A man in love

Scholars seem to agree that the Romantic poet, John Keats, had a rather problematic attitude towards women. Though he was attracted to young women, he was also repelled by what he considered to be their flirtatious and untrustworthy behaviour. In particular, the poet had a long, difficult relationship with his beloved, Fanny Brawne. Keats's letters show that he often worried about whether Fanny Brawne really loved him and that he was jealous of any attention she received from other men. Simultaneously he fretted about being trapped in their relationship:

'Ask yourself my love whether you are not very cruel to have so entrammelled me, so destroyed my freedom'.

And love itself, he sometimes described in his letters as an affliction: 'A man in love I do think cuts the sorryest figure in the world'.

Though, as we will see, this poem can be read in many ways, and although not all its mysteries can be neatly resolved, at its simplest level, dressed in medieval garb, supernaturalied and mythologised, featuring a character entrammelled and imprisoned, *La Belle Dame Sans Merci* expresses Keats's ambivalent feelings about the power of love, sex and women.

A few years before completing *La Belle Dame* Keats had written in *Edymonion* that 'A thing of beauty is a joy forever', one that will 'keep a bower quiet for us, and a sleep / full of sweet dreams'. His *Ode to a Grecian Urn* concludes with the resounding declaration that 'beauty is truth, truth beauty' and Keats's poetry, as a whole, can be seen as a quest after beauty. But *La Belle Dame Sans Merci* upsets his equation of beauty with truth: Certainly the titular character is beautiful, but the knight is mistaken when he thinks she loves him 'true'. Rather than bringing him peace, the knight is left the sorriest figure, 'haggard and woebegone', 'alone and palely loitering'. Beauty in this poem is entrancing, captivating. But it is also deceptive, dangerous, draining. Perhaps this is why, simultaneously some sort of goddess and demon, the figure of La Belle Dame cast such a powerful spell on Keats's imagination.

A safe distance?

Keats's ballad features two narrators - a frame narrator who begins the poem and asks questions, and a knight who takes up the narration in the fourth stanza. Mysteriously the frame narrator disappears from the scene, diminishing to only a faint linguistic echo in the last stanza, leaving a lingering sense of incompleteness to the poem. This begs the question, <u>what is the function of the frame narrator and why does he, or she, vanish</u>? Firstly, the narrator twice asks questions of the knight; what is wrong with him and why he is wandering about like a lost soul. Use of the apostrophe, 'O', implies concern for the knight, indicating that the narrator is not merely an objective or disinterested observer - somehow they are emotionally involved in the poem's events. As well as setting the scene and witnessing the knight's anguished state, the narrator also seeks an explanation for the pale knight's strange, wandering behaviour.

The literal minded among us may wonder what exactly the narrator was doing near this silent, withered lake, where he [or she] happens upon the 'haggard' knight. Perhaps Keats is suggesting that the narrator is potentially another victim of La Belle Dame Sans Merci, somebody who has also strayed from the safety of civilisation and from the masculine sphere of action. Just as the knight is warned by the dead men, so the knight warns the narrator. The narrator seeks answers from the knight perhaps so that [s]he can avoid meeting the same fate. If we accept this reading, Keats uses the narrator to amplify the story, to suggest that there is something universal in the pattern of seduced and betrayed men. Unwarned, the narrator might have followed the knight who has, in his turn, followed the 'pale warriors' to the elfin grot. Initially it is as if the narrator is asking us their questions, which places us, albeit momentarily, in the position of the knight. Hence the poem implies the reader too can be drawn into its seductive narrative.

There is another way of looking at this. As we've said, on one level Keats's poem is about the dangers of falling in love with a beautiful, but untrustworthy woman and dramatises his fear that women may betray men.

At the heart of the poem there appears a pretty straightforward story of a short-lived love affair followed by a break-up. However, Keats wishes to explore and understand his feelings by getting some perspective on them, examining them from a distance. Hence he supernaturalises and medievalises the story, transforming it into a timeless myth. The use of the two narrators reflects the way in which the poet tries to distance himself from his experience, adopting the seemingly safe position of frame narrator as well as of the armoured and armed figure of a knight. The fact that he slips so seamlessly from outside observer to protagonist suggests the power of the story to dissolve such defensive strategies, to draw Keats in. Similarly, the knight's armour offers him no protection against the bewitching Belle Dame.

The knight

The transition from narrator to character could have been indicated through the use of speech marks. Keats employs these to indicate the speech of the woman and the dead men too. So why not use them when the knight speaks? If the poet had wanted to distinguish clearly between the two speakers he could also have given them different language, in terms of register, vocabulary and rhythms. Taken together, it seems that Keats wished to deliberately blur any distinction between the two characters. They are either two potential victims, or essentially two versions of the same person, one before and the other after encountering La Belle Dame.

Obviously the knight fits with the Romantic medieval atmosphere of the poem. The medieval setting also implies that this is an archetypal story, a timeless pattern of behaviour repeated eternally. This would all be true if the character were a wandering minstrel, or such like. A 'knight', however, has connotations of an ideal man: nobility of character, masculine strength and power, action, heroism, the highest standards of chivalry etc. In medieval Romances knights fight and vanquish monsters in order to win the hand of beautiful, virtuous maidens. In Keats's twist of the story, the beautiful, virtuous maiden turns out to be the monster. And if a knight and other noble characters, such as kings and princes, can be so easily undone what chance for ordinary mortals? Or, indeed, for poets?

The effect La Belle Dame has on the knight is specific:

1. He loses blood and looks ill; he is exhausted, enfeebled and feels 'forlorn': 'O what can ail thee'…'fever'…'palely'…'haggard'…'woebegone'.

2. He is isolated ['alone'] and stripped of his active, heroic role - he is away from battle, aimlessly 'loitering'. He has become the wandering ghost of his former self. Once a man of noble action, all he can do now is to pass on his dreadful warning.

3. Moreover, his appearance suggests that the knight has been emasculated. Both similes in the third stanza use flowers associated with feminine beauty, the lily and the rose. The process of his loss of male power can be traced through the verbs used in the middle section of the poem. On first meeting La Belle Dame, the knight appears to be in control. He is the active subject of the verbs 'I met', 'I made', 'I set'. These three little, simple monosyllabic verbs, coming at the start of three successive stanzas, summarise a swift, bold courtship. The gallant knight sweeps the lady off her feet and onto the back of his horse. Like Caesar, he came he saw and he swiftly conquered. All the lady does is make a 'sweet moan' and 'sing'.

Before becoming entrapped by La Belle Dame the knight makes her presents, love tokens of a 'garland' and a 'bracelet' and, despite her saying nothing, he confidently reads her looks as showing 'she did love'. There's a subtly disturbing, ambiguous quality to 'and sure in language strange she said'. If the language is 'strange', or foreign, how can he be 'sure' of what she is really saying?

The sixth stanza begins the reversal in power. Agency of the verbs switches to La Belle Dame. The knight becomes their passive object. He is lulled into being the submissive partner:

- 'she found me'
- 'she took me'
- 'she lulled me'

Fed and 'lulled' to sleep, he is further unmanned and diminished by being infantilised. Only in his unquiet dream does he escape the enchantment. Even here he is a passive witness rather than active agent. Significantly, Keats uses the same verb to forge a link between the knight and the narrator. Both see pale victims of La Belle Dame, both are warned of her seductive, but treacherous beauty.

Imagination, in the form of a dream, warns the knight of his fate as another victim of the mysterious enchantress. When he wakes the 'elfin grot' has disappeared and he is alone on a hill. What would you do in this situation? Run as fast as your legs would take you, back to battle and the manly world of knights, I warrant. Warned, why then doesn't this knight escape? For one thing he seems to have lost his 'pacing steed' and is now on foot. Clearly this symbolises a loss of status and masculine power. Though he appears to be alive, he also seems trapped by his experience, doomed to repeat it as a story. Or perhaps he's so pale and haggard, so withered because now this knight is now just a ghost, unable to leave the place where he lost his life.

La Belle Dame

Unless, rather perversely, we take the narrator to be female, the poem is told entirely from a male perspective. Notably, La Belle Dame Sans Merci never has the chance to express her opinions, or to explain her motivation. Her voice is silenced. <u>Who, or what, is this beautiful 'faery' woman?</u>

We know some key things about her appearance: she's 'full beautiful', with 'long' hair and 'wild' eyes. Keats emphasises this last feature through repetition of the same adjective in stanza eight, 'her wild, wild eyes'. The woman is characterised only through the vague generalities of her physical attractiveness and her untamed otherness. We learn that she's also exotic, non-human, supernatural in some way; 'a faery's child' she lives in an 'elfin grot'. Her home is away from towns and people, somewhere in the wild ['the meads']. Her appearance suggests a lost damsel from a Romance story. Initially she's docile and virtually mute, just making 'sweet' moans. And she seems extraordinarily easily wooed. All it takes is a few 'garlands' and she's ready to be whisked off on the knight's horse; hardly the behaviour of a civilised lady of virtue. Her virtual silence and easy compliance with the knight's wishes seem to make her more attractive to him. From his male perspective she's a perfect fantasy woman. The knight hardly has to do anything to persuade this beautiful woman to leap into his arms.

Peculiarly, when she gets the knight home to her 'grot' she just cries and 'sigh'd full sore'. <u>How are we to read this weeping?</u> Regret at what she is going to do? Regret that, like the knight, she is trapped in this narrative pattern? Or are her tears meant to signal her deceitfulness? Vulnerability a subtle weapon to make the knight lower his guard even further?

Sweet tooth

After seeming entirely submissive at first, suddenly La Belle Dame takes control. She feeds the knight, as if fattening him up with tasty, exotic, heavenly food - 'relish sweet', 'honey wild' and 'manna dew'. The food can also have another symbolic significance. According to the critic, Lionel Trilling, 'for Keats, the luxury of food is connected with, and in a sense gives place to, the luxury of sexuality'. In other words, eating fruit is coded reference to sexual intercourse. If we accept this, then the poem dramatizes Keats's fear that love and intercourse might lead to some sort of entrapment and loss of male power. And in this reading, the lady behaves with a liberty that would have been deeply shocking to a polite nineteenth century audience. Then she sends him to sleep. Here she takes on the role of a mother, feeding and putting a child to bed. <u>Does this make La Belle Dame more disconcerting?</u> A fairy lover/ goddess/ enchantress, but also a demon/ inverted mother/ witch figure.

The phrase 'in thrall' signals that she has made the knight her slave or servant, diminishing him even further. We also learn that many men have been victims and that she has a name: La Belle Dame Sans Merci. <u>Can we presume she must be French?</u> Either the whole poem is set in France [but the characters fortunately speak English] or else she is French and foreign to the knight. Perhaps this adds to her impression of exotic otherness. Written not longer after England had been at War with France, La Belle Dame's Frenchness might also make her seem a more threatening or symbolic figure. Clearly the repetition of the adjective 'pale', used about both the knight and the other 'pale...death-pale' victims, indicates

that they have lost blood. In this sense La Belle Dame seems to be some sort of Gothic blood-sucker, a vampire, perhaps; beautiful, predatory, deadly. That would fit with her hard-to-categorise quality. Whatever symbolic significance we assign her, she remains a fictional version of Fanny Brawne.

Unmasking La Belle Dame

More metaphorically, she could be a personification of death, or disease. Bringing 'fever' and 'anguish', weakness and 'paleness', she leaves her victim listless and forlorn [and perhaps also dead!]. Arguably she is a symbol for the irresistible power of tuberculosis, the disease that killed Keats and several members of his immediate family. Some critics have also suggested she could symbolise drug addiction; we know that at one point during his illness Keats's friends were appalled to find he had been dosing himself with laudanum.

More radically still she could be read as a symbol of imagination, beauty or even of poetry itself. The manly knight falls in love with the woman and turns a melancholy, emasculated poet! Alas! Certainly Keats sometimes worried that imaginative adventure, the intoxication of poetry, might be a way of avoiding engaging properly and actively with the real world. In this interpretation La Belle Dame is the goddess muse of poetry who enchants and enslaves the will of the male poet.

Or if we go back to her Frenchness, La Belle Dame could symbolise the revolutionary ideas that drove the French Revolution. Many of the Romantic poets were captivated by these ideas and some championed the cause of revolution - Wordsworth and Blake were notable enthusiasts. However, the aftermath of the revolution was bloody and chaotic, as one form of tyranny was replaced by another just as virulent. During the 'Reign of Terror' thousands of people were publicly executed and hopes for a better, fairer, more just society were swept away by a rising tide of blood-letting.

All these readings are plausible. The great thing with symbols is they can pack in many meanings inside one image – and still retain their mystery. It is part of what makes Keats's poem so captivating.

A poetic spell

Keats's poem doesn't just describe an enchantment; it weaves its own spell on the reader. Mainly this is achieved through setting, repetition, adaptation of the ballad form and the poem's overall structure. The setting is sketched in a few quick strokes:

'The sedge has wither'd from the lake
and no birds sing'

A tense and eerie atmosphere is conjured by the silence and we may wonder why no birds are singing - a notorious sign of danger. The verb, 'withered' suggests decay and links the landscape to the knight on whose cheek a 'fading rose/ fast withereth too'. Keats uses pathetic fallacy here so that the landscape seems to reflect the knight's mood and mindset. As with the narrator and other dead men, this device suggests more is at stake than the fate of a single knight.

With one exception, the conjunction 'and' is used in every stanza. Sentences are organised in a simple narrative fashion: This happened and then this happened and then this happened. The absence of subordinating conjunctions indicates that Keats does not explain the events, just sets them out before us, so that they retain their mystery. The gently insistent repetition of diction, syntax, and metre establishes an incantatory rhythm. The pulse is also muted - there are few emphatically stressed syllables. The repetition of the muted rhythm further enhances the trance-like feel. Each stanza ends with a full stop and follows the same pattern. Hence, though the story moves onwards, there is a counter force of stillness and stasis.

Keats also adapts the ballad metre. Conventionally a ballad is written in quatrains of alternating four beat [tetrameters] and three beats [trimeters] often in iambic feet. The poet stretches the second lines into tetrameter: 'Alone and palely loitering'; 'So haggard and so woebegone'; 'With anguish moist and fever dew'.

Ti-TUM ti-TUM ti-TUM ti-TUM

And he docks a beat from the fourth lines. Look, for example, at 'and no birds sing', 'and made sweet moan', 'on the cold hill's side', which all end heavily with three stressed monosyllables in a row. At other times, he trims the last line of the quatrain back further: 'with kisses four', 'hath thee in thrall', 'a faery's song' are dimeters – just two beats. The unbalancing, stretching and cutting of the form creates tension at the end of each stanza, a feeling of being brought up short, or something being not quite right or as expected. Another way of thinking of the metre is in terms of rising and falling. Traditionally the second line has the falling quality of a trimeter following a tetrameter. By lengthening this line Keats has three lines with a rising quality, hence accentuating the dying fall of the final line of each stanza.

Overall the poem has a cyclical structure, with the last stanza's language echoing the first two. This link between the start and end highlights the interesting passage of time in the poem. The first two stanzas and the final one are in the present tense, 'ail', 'loitering', whereas the story the knight tells is in the past tense, 'I met', 'her hair was'. It is almost as if after the knight has told his story we re-enter the same moment, as he answers the narrator's question.

Working together the various aspects conjure a feeling of suspended animation, of time stuck, held and halted, which further strengthens the poem's hypnotic, haunting spell.

'Crunching' a poem entails reducing each line to the single most important word.

La Belle crunched:

KNIGHT-AT-ARMS – ALONE – WITHER'D – NO – AIL – WOEBEGONE – FULL – DONE – LILY – FEVER – FADING – WITHERETH – LADY – FAERY'S – HAIR – EYES – GARLAND – FRAGRANT – LOVE – MOAN – STEED – NOTHING – SING – FAERY'S – RELISH – MANNA – STRANGE – TRUE – ELFIN – WEPT – WILD – KISSES – LULLED – WOE – DREAM'D – COLD – PRINCES – DEATH-PALE – BELLE – THRALL – STARVED – WARNING – AWOKE – HILL – SOJOURN – ALONE – WITHER'D – SING

NB
Perhaps we have overstated one reading; that the knight has been trapped and possibly even killed by the La Belle Dame. Another possibility is that he is so pale and feverish because he feels guilt at what has happened in the 'elfin grot'. Perhaps La Belle Dame is more innocent that we'd supposed, perhaps she is even the victim.

Joanna Baillie, *A Child to His Sick Grandfather*

The seemingly universally liked and admired Scottish poet Joanna Baillie [1762-1851] was one of the very few pre-twentieth century female writers famous and celebrated in her own times. A prolific playwright as well as a poet, Baillie was also a philanthropist who gave half the earnings from her literary works to charity and a supporter of progressive causes, such as attempts to improve the lives of child chimney sweeps.

Baillie's playwriting skills are put to good use in this dramatic monologue written in the voice of a child. Neither child nor grandfather is given a name which suggests they are intended to be universal types. Additionally, though the title reveals the child is male, their caring, nursing qualities are typically female virtues and their age is uncertain. A few words here and there, such as 'ne'ertheless', 'weal', 'aye' and 'partlet', help create the sense both of a speaking voice and perhaps of Scottishness. Though it is skilfully strung along the fretwork of metre, noticeably Baillie's language is very simple, comprising of common words used with straightforward syntax and sentence construction. Take the fifth stanza, for example. Of the 44 words 41 are monosyllables and the other three 'again', 'quiet', 'softly' are hardly complex. Another example would be the prevalence of the simplest possible conjunction 'and' in the poem. In the fourth stanza, four lines in a row begin with this conjunction indicating that the clauses are connected in the simplest possible way. Homespun vocabulary is also employed literally; figurative language is entirely absent from the poem. If we recall that Aristotle believed the genius of a poet depended on their facility with metaphor, it's a bold stroke to write a whole poem in such a plain style and without a single metaphor.

We could compare Baillie's use of straightforward vocabulary with Barrett Browning's in sonnet 43. Both poets employ simple words – Barrett Browning's poem opens with a run of monosyllables, 'How do I love thee? Let me count the ways' and the extreme simplicity of the language is a testament to the truth of the emotions being expressed. Baillie's choice of simple language has a similar function; the child is expressing their feelings in transparent language. There is no artifice or deception here; the plain language attests to the honesty of the speaker. Of course, the simplicity of the language also helps to make the voice of the child narrator convincing. But, whereas Baillie maintains this style throughout her dramatic monologue, Barrett Browning soon begins to use simple words in complex ways through figurative imagery.

Romantics

A contemporary of Wordsworth [1770-1850] Baillie seems to have shared some of the artistic principles of the Romantic poets. Firstly, her subject is an ordinary child talking on an ordinary subject, relations within a family. There is

nothing elevated, sophisticated or especially 'poetic' about this subject. Secondly, Baillie applies Wordsworth's advice in rejecting the previous generation of poets inflated and decorative language in favour of language that is much closer to ordinary speech.

Thirdly, the Romantics were the first writers to make childhood and children a distinct subject, seeing the former as a special, significant time that shaped adulthood, and the latter as innocents uncorrupted by the evils of society. For the Romantics, citizens of cultivated society could and should learn from the wisdom of children and from the example of the often hard lives of ordinary rustic folk. Lastly, Romantic poetry was poetry of the heart, its subject was often emotions and it characteristically aimed to have a more emotional than intellectual effect on its readers.

The old man and the child

The two characters in the poem are presented sympathetically. The emphasis in the portrait of the Grandfather is on his physical weakness and age. He is 'old' and 'frail', bent-over, he has trouble walking, his beard [a traditional symbol of manliness] is 'lank' and 'thin', he's bald,

his cheeks are 'wan' and 'hollow'. We also learn that he is well-liked, 'everybody' is 'sad', housewives brew 'potions', others ask after the state of his health and 'good men kneel' in prayer to aid his recovery. He also had a strong influence on the speaker, tenderly stroking their head and telling him 'how good children did'. The fact that he is addressed both as 'grand-dad' and as 'dad' implies that he may perform the role of both these figures for the child.

The child speaker is also presented as a virtuous, kindly character. In particular they show a ready sympathy with the suffering of their grandfather. In the third stanza, for example, the two exclamation marks signal this sympathetic feeling. We are encouraged to feel pity for the child when they express their fear for the death of their dear relative: 'You'll not die and leave us then?' The fact that the question is couched as a statement poignantly conveys the unwillingness of the child to accept this will happen. Moreover, the speaker tries to galvanise and comfort their grandfather, shifting into the imperative to implore him to 'rouse up' and later trying to entertain him with stories. In addition, this ideal grandchild patiently puts aside time 'to sit with' their  dying relative, physically supports him into dinner and constantly reassures him that he is beloved. The boy's care is also evident from the fact that he sits beside his grandfather's bed when the old man is asleep and will 'aye' [always] be near when he awakes. His tirelessness is also suggested by the length of the poem and the repeated pattern of each stanza. The fact that adult readers can work out before the child that despite all the speaker's sterling efforts this grandfather probably won't recover makes the poem more poignant. This is particularly the case in the last stanza when the child doesn't seem fully aware of the fact that the grandfather has probably died.

Foreshadowing

Baillie's verse form sets up the expectation of this outcome from the start. Each stanza is a sestet arranged into three couplets [the couplet form being an obvious choice for a poem about two people, of course]. The dominant metre is tetrameter, sometimes called common metre, and this ticks away pretty consistently throughout the poem. Take, for example, the first two lines of the second stanza:

You **used** to **smile** and **stroke** my **head**
And **tell** me **how** good **child**ren **did**

However, the last of each stanza is shorter, six rather than eight syllables, three rather than four stresses. In other words, one beat is missing from each of the last lines, so that each stanza ends with this loss and, rhythmically, with a dying fall. The effect is heightened as the poem progresses by the frequent use of half-rhymes rather than full rhymes in the final couplets – 'led – dad'; 'head –dad'.

The last line of the poem uses the very simplest language possible: 'you do not hear me dad' and is, as we've said, made moving through the implication that the old man has died. Baillie's skill with metre adds to the effect. The stresses in this line fall on 'do', 'hear' and 'dad'. The two subjects in the poem, the speaker and the grandfather are placed in unstressed positions and hence subtly diminished.

After her death Baillie's plays fell out of fashion and rarely have they been revived. Tastes change, of course, and literary fashions move on. In its own time *A Child to his Sick Grandfather* probably was radical in its choice of subject matter and its plain language. However, to modern ears the poem might sound a little sentimental. The grandfather and the child are both presented in a rather gentle soft-focus and this, arguably, makes it hard for us to really believe in them as real individuals. What do you think? Is the poem charming and moving or trite and sentimental, or something else?

A Child to his Sick Grandfather crunched:

[Due to the length of this poem we've produced a crunchier crunch.]

OLD – SAD – BESIDE – THIN – WAN – LOVE – EACH – PRAYERS – AILING – DIE – SOFTLY – AYE – KINDLY – TALK – TALE – THINK – DAD.

Lord Byron, *She Walks in Beauty*

Lord Byron, or George Gordon Byron, is a love poet with a notorious reputation. Famously labelled 'mad, bad and dangerous to know', Byron was renowned for his flamboyance, condemned for his immoral lifestyle and chased for his huge debts. Following rumours of incest with his half-sister, he fled England, exiling himself in Europe and he died of a fever in Greece aged 36. During his life he was one of the second generation of Romantic poets, which included Percy Bysshe Shelley and John Keats.

This poem is famous for its rich lyricism compressed into such a short work. Byron's most famous other poems, such as *Don Juan* are epically long, but here we find complex language and imagery distilled into a pithy snapshot of a strange, dreamlike, entrancing female. Like Keats's *La Belle Dame*, it's not really a love poem; it's more of an infatuation or obsession poem. The fascination with which this woman is described is remarkably similar to those descriptions of nature's beauty which so captivated Romantic poets. More particularly, the Romantic poets' idea of nature is that it can sometimes lure you in with chilling and otherworldly power, just like the woman does in *She walks in Beauty*. She's made into a 'type' by the vision of the poem's enraptured speaker, a generic desirable goal made more of an achievement through presenting her as distant, unattainable, mysterious.

Superficiality

Whilst it's true to say that the poem has lots of superficial elements, it's also true that it makes the most of these. Superficiality shines through the language. The curiously generic description of the woman is made delicate and one-dimensional by the fact that the speaker refuses to talk of anything else. The perfect metre of the opening lines, in particular, signals a surface-level perfection that can be delicately wobbled or disrupted, like the glassy surface of a pond in the wind- 'she <u>walks</u> in <u>beauty</u>, <u>like</u> the <u>night</u>/ of <u>cloud</u>less <u>climes</u> and <u>starry</u> <u>skies</u>'.

'Pure', 'cloudless', 'tender', 'sweet', 'at peace', 'innocent', this is a woman that does nothing but smile and be a vessel for grace and physical attractiveness- her only facial expressions are rather blank [like 'thoughts serenely sweet express'] and the time when her face appears at all engaged is where she has 'smiles that win' to remember 'days in goodness spent'. Those in the 19th century just as much as those in the 21st century knew perfectly well that a paragon such as this did not exist- Byron is painting with the literary brushes of sensuousness and physical experience to create the feelings of awe and perhaps real reverence for an idealised object, not a real woman.

Byron deliberately doesn't create a complex and multifaceted character, nor does he provide a snapshot of a heroine from one of his epic poems. This is a different exercise- he capitalises on the short structure he is using to paint a static image, suspended in time. An admirer of the Augustan poets Pope and Dryden, characteristically in this poetry Byron was a satirist. He could be withering, for instance, about his fellow Romantic Poets; habitually he referred to the Lake poets, Wordsworth and Coleridge, as the 'pond poets' and rather rudely renamed the former Turdsworth. <u>Is there any part of this poem that comes across as satirical to you?</u>

Keep your distance?

Byron was a widely-travelled man, especially with regard to the Far East; it is easy to see the sensory impact of rich and foreign lands on his work. Nowadays the description 'oriental' isn't really used, because the root of the word suggests that the east revolves round the West [and we know perfectly well that the West isn't the centre of the universe!] However, Byron uses language that would have typically conjured up images of the exotic, of the foreign, of the 'other', in a world where trading passages made exposure to the Far East increasingly easy, and where the East was seen as a world of danger, intrigue and dark magic.

The woman described in the poem is described as the 'night'. This is curious as the night is something that co-exists with day, but never coincides with it, shrouded by mystery and revolving as the dark face of the Earth- always chasing the sun. Byron talks about her delicate, ideal balance by describing 'one shade the more, one ray the less'- like the encroaching of night upon day. Like a pair of compasses, the woman occupies the place of night; removed, and slightly out of reach, yet always faithfully revolving around the light. Perhaps the speaker of the poem takes the place of the figure always separated from this mysterious woman, but always part of her presence; this would give the impression that the woman is removed and unattainable, and we know how much male love poets like talking about women who are aloof and unattainable!

Another interesting aspect of the woman's appearance is the emphasis on her darkness and her mystique. She is at once 'all that's best of dark and bright', at once being two things- seductive because of her glittering 'smiles that win, the tints that glow' but cloaked in 'shade' that makes her all the more alluring. Her 'raven tress' and the 'starry skies' indicate that impact of Orientalism on Byron's work- the attraction to something that is exotic and strange, and the fetishisation of other cultures because they seem so far away from our own. Women from other countries, especially Asia, were frequently fetishized in this way to create the narrative of their unattainability and therefore heighten the difficulty [and hence reward] of the 'conquest'.

For an example of how the Romantic poets in particular used Orientalism to aestheticise those from eastern countries, have a look at *Kubla Khan* by Coleridge. The paradise there, 'where blossomed many an incense-bearing tree', creates that same kind of still, perfect world that Byron's 'mysterious girl' inhabits. She seems to radiate from with, 'softly lighten[ed] o'er her face', 'the tints that glow', 'mellowed to that tender light'.

Do you think the speaker is interested in speaking to this woman or is he happy to have her kept at a distance? Why?

Light and darkness

It's an interesting study of subjectivity that this woman can only be seen in the context of light, and is completely defined by how she is shaded- 'one shade the more, one ray the less'. The night that she is compared to is itself defined by 'starry skies'. She is made purely aesthetic, purely a physical being, by the fact that she can only be seen in light and has no obvious internal worth or complexity. Ironically, though she does not speak, her body speaks for her. Her cheeks or brow, in particular are described, somewhat improbably as 'eloquent', although the adjective could also be read as describing her smiles. Apparently her mind is also  at peace [so basically there's nothing going on in her head] and her heart's 'love is innocent' [so she's never experienced any kind of relationship].

Alternatively, though she is defined by light, she can also be seen by it even when it is dark, like a beacon in 'the night / of cloudless climes'. She seems to have an inner radiance, generating her own light and this draws men to her, like a beacon. Or perhaps like moths to a flame. The fact that she remains removed throughout the poem suggests her inner light is like a lighthouse, warning ships away from a rocky shore. Is it possible that beneath the apparent serene beauty of this woman, hidden under the elegant and smooth poetic metre, and tucked inside the seemingly flattering imagery lurks something darker, dangerous and more threatening? The idea that a woman's beauty is dangerous is, of course, a common thread running through literature, but especially so at the time of the Romantic Movement. As Keats's *La Belle Dame Sans Merci* illustrates the vampire genre really took root by making female sexuality demonic and otherworldly. <u>Can Byron's lady be read in the same way as some sort of femme fatale? Is the poem the dreamy expression of a bewitched potential victim?</u>

This woman isn't blonde and beautiful, like an innocent child or angel. Rather she is dark [which brings into play the obvious negative connotations of 'darkness'] and 'of the night', a meaning which would have had much more impact on Byron's contemporary audience [particularly given his own liaisons with sex workers and other sexual encounters that would have been deemed immoral or illegal at the time]. Her hair is described as 'raven' black and ravens are, of course, associated with death and evil. Perhaps her description also implies innate sexual knowledge, her 'winning' smile luring the speaker [and the reader in] to her trust and affection.

In the end, though, this reading feels like forcing the poem into something it isn't. The significance of the various references to darkness in the poem is not due to connotations of evil or death, but rather that the lady is an ideal because in her the opposites of dark and light are perfectly reconciled. Yes, the poet is entranced by this figure and she does remain remote and rather ethereal. But there's nothing really convincing to suggest that her beauty and goodness is a trap luring in the besotted male.

What is certain in this poem is that the speaker uses the technique of synecdoche [using a part of something to describe the whole]. The only physical things we learn about the woman is a lot about her eyes, her face, and her dark hair, but the rest of her is presumably shrouded in the same darkness as the night which imposes as shade to make 'one ray the less'.

She Walks in Beauty crunched:

WALKS – BEAUTY – NIGHT – STARRY – DARK – BRIGHT – EYES –
TENDER – HEAVEN – SHADE – RAY – GRACE – RAVEN –
LIGHTENS – SERENELY – PURE – DEAR – ELOQUENT – SMILES –
GOODNESS – PEACE – LOVE – INNOCENT

William Wordsworth, *A Complaint*

Language really used by men

What do the following words from Wordsworth's poem have in common?

fountain	bounty	ago	moments	business	taking	happy
above	consecrated	murmuring	sparkling	living	comfortless	
hidden	matter	waters	obscurity	silence		

Furthermore, what do the words in the following, even more select, selection have in common?

Consecrated   murmuring   comfortless

Yes, the first is a list of polysyllabic words and the second a list of words with three syllables. This illustrates how the majority of Wordsworth's poem, like Joanna Baillie's, is composed of very simple monosyllables. Indeed, four lines are composed entirely of monosyllables, including the opening and the closing ones. In terms of vocabulary, syntax and semantics language cannot get much simpler or more direct than this poem's opening declarative line:

'There is a change – and I am poor'.

And yet this simplicity communicates powerfully. The hyphen in the middle of the line is a small bridge spanning a chasm, a chasm between a before and an after, a space of time during which everything has changed and changed 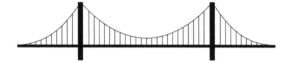 for the far worse. The bluntness of the language conveys the suddenness of this change as well as the sense that the poet is still trying to deal with it.

Though this is an extreme example, such simplicity of vocabulary, or what is technically called diction, is characteristic of Wordsworth's poetry and of Romantic poetry as a whole. Romantic poets believed that the language of poetry had become inflated, artificial and overly stylised and that it needed stripping back to something closer to the language of ordinary speech. Their aim was for an intensification or purification of this ordinary speech. There was a progressive political as well as an aesthetic dimension to this preference, as Romantic poets sought to enlarge the audience of poetry from a small educated elite to all literate people. In a preface to the 1805 edition of *The Lyrical Ballads* he wrote with his friend Samuel Taylor Coleridge shortly before *A Complaint,* Wordsworth wrote that his poems would dispense with the 'gaudiness and inane phraseology of many modern writers' and take as their topic 'incidents and situations from common life' which he would render in the 'language really used by men'.

If the diction and syntax of Wordsworth's poem are straightforward, so too are the small group of figurative images. The image of love being like a 'fountain' is easily understood, with its connotations of bubbling energy, generosity and precious, life-giving vibrancy. In any case, Wordsworth ensures we arrive at this sort of interpretation by referring to the fountain as 'sparkling' like jewels and as 'living love'. Similarly, we have few problems understanding the image of the heart as a house with its own 'door' or the  personification of the heart itself as almost an autonomous 'fond' agent. The central switch in the poem is from the metaphor of the fountain to that of a 'well', another source of water, but one that is underground, below the surface and static. As with the fountain, Wordsworth gives readers a semantic nudge by telling us that the well is 'comfortless' and 'hidden', 'deep' and never 'dry', remote and silent.

In short, Wordsworth seems to achieve his aim to communicate his experience and in particular, his feelings, in a comprehensible, unaffected and direct way. However, for a poem conveying the distress and desolation of loss *A Complaint* is remarkably orderly and composed.

Emotion recollected in tranquility

The poem is made up of three regular sestets following the same rhyme scheme and metrical pattern. In each stanza four cross-rhymed lines are followed by a couplet. Neatly this form runs counter to what the words say, as sonically the rhymes come closer together at the end of each stanza. The lines tick over like a smooth engine in regular iambic tetrameter. For example, 'your **love** hath **been**, not **long** ago'. The combination of the regular metre and down-to-earth, mundane vocabulary means it's inevitable that function words often carry stress in a way that would have been judged crude and inelegant by a previous generation of poets. For example, in the first stanza there's a run of insignificant words 'is', 'I', 'been', 'at', 'was', 'did', 'its', 'or' all taking a metrical stress. Whether you judge this poor poetic craftsmanship or a clear indication of Wordsworth's deflation of poetic pomposity is up to you.

All the lines follow this unruffled pattern, apart from two. Clearly this draws our attention to those two lines:

1. 'A **foun**tain **at** my **fond heart's door**'
2. 'Of **mur**muring, **spar**kling, **living love**'

In the first example, although, like all the other lines bar one, the line has eight syllables, it can be scanned as having an extra, fifth stress; surely 'heart' is important enough a word to demand emphasis. Such a reading adds a weightiness to the end of the line. However, the line can also be scanned as a regular iambic tetrameter, in which case 'heart' is diminished as a word in a way that, considering the poem's theme of a lost intensity of love, is both fitting and poignant. The second example is the only line that has an extra, ninth syllable. This helps both elongate the line and to draw attention the run of three present participles. Moreover, it's the adjective 'murmuring' that bucks the regular pattern, highlighting how the fountain of love was like an intimate speaker, communicating gently with the poet, a significant contrast to the 'silence' of the well.

As with the metre, so with the rhymes. Most are full, masculine rhymes that slot seamlessly into place. This even sonic pattern is only disrupted a little in the penultimate line where 'obscurity' doesn't quite harmonise with its pair, 'and never dry', creating a suitable slight dissonance. Wordsworth draws on the etymology of 'obscurity' here. From its Old French origins, the word carries the sense of gloom and darkness, another contrast with the 'sparkling' fountain.

Famously Wordsworth referred to poetry as expressing 'emotion recollected in tranquility'. The danger of this is that could to be a potential mismatch between feeling and treatment: However tempestuous or violent the emotion, it is recalled from a temporal and emotional distance, from a state of unruffled calmness.  Potentially this could lead to a weakening of the force with which the emotion is conveyed. Certainly, in its orderly, even metre and regular rhymes, *A Complaint* might be in danger of falling into this trap. And if the poem doesn't really convey the speaker's distress doubts may arise about the true depth of these emotions.

A playwright once explained how it took them several plays to realise that it was more dramatically effective to have a character bravely holding back tears than having them cry. The former creates a tension the latter lacks. Another way of looking at the orderliness of Wordsworth's is as an analogue for putting on a brave face, for showing fortitude and keeping going, for keeping difficult emotions in check. For there to be this dramatic tension, beneath the surface of the calm facade and steadfastness, there must be signs of emotional disturbance. For evidence of this tension, we could point to the irregular metrical lines we've already noted and the sonically awkward, not fully resolved penultimate rhyme. But the major indication of strong feelings held in check by the frame of the poem is the punctuation.

Agents of fragmentation

If you were very meticulous and systematic you could count the number of each type of punctuation in the poem. But, take even a quick look at and you can see there's an awful lot of punctuation for a short poem and also quite a range too. Two exclamation marks, three semi-colons and three question marks, no less than five dashes, or hyphens, and a very liberal smattering of commas and full stops. At one point Wordsworth even uses two punctuation marks in a row, a comma and a dash. What do these punctuation marks do? Often they work as caesuras, breaking up the pattern of the verse, making the movement of the lines hesitant, uncertain and choppy. Look through the lines and you'll see many of them have these breaks. The start of the final stanza is a particularly good example of this principle of fragmentation: There are only four words before the first hyphen breaks up the line and creates a momentary pause; only four words follow before there's another pause; four more words and then there's a double pause with both a comma and a dash; just three words precede a colon, and then just two words 'what matter' [just one stressed beat] before the question mark.

Whereas the diction, rhyme and metre knit the poem together to make a seamless whole, the punctuation pulls the words and voice of the poem apart, fracturing it, isolating short phrase into fragments, making the whole piece move with a broken, hesitant, distressed rhythm. For a poem about the break-up of a relationship this is, of course, entirely fitting.

A Complaint crunched:

CHANGE – BEEN – FOUNTAIN – FLOW – HEED – NEED – HAPPY – BLISS – CONSECRATED – LOVE – WHAT – COMFORTLESS – DEEP – NEVER – SLEEP – OBSCURITY – CHANGE – POOR

NB

What sort of a relationship might Wordsworth be describing? The poem is ambiguous. Even the title, for example, could be read in terms of the modem meaning or the word 'complaint' as being a protest against something that has gone wrong, but, in this poetic context, it also recalls the older usage of the word to indicate a lament. And a protest and a lament are different things. And who is being addressed? Is the addressee an ex-lover, perhaps? If so, the language is rather chaste and desexualised - the addressee seems to be more a source of inspiration than an object of passion. Though Wordsworth does not narrow the poem to this particular context, scholars suggest that the addressee was, in fact, Coleridge, Wordsworth's one time close friend and collaborator with whom he had fallen out.

Thomas Hardy, *Neutral Tones*

Long, cold shadows

How do we look back on lost love, on relationships we thought were going to endure but where love did not last the test of time? Are such experiences consigned to the ash heap of history, never to be thought of again, or does something about them linger in our imagination and haunt our present? Hardy's poetry is preoccupied with ghosts, sometimes literal, but more often metaphorical spectres of the past that disturb and oppress the troubled memories of his poems' speakers. In *Neutral Tones* we see how a failed relationship casts its long and cold shadow across the narrator's subsequent life like a stone dropped into the centre of a pond whose ripple travels out to the water's far edges.

Titles are nearly always significant signposts for interpreting poems and the title of this poem is no exception. On one level, a 'neutral tone' refers to any of the chromatic colours - white, black or grey - that, scientifically speaking, are not actually colours due to their lack of hue. Hardy's poem is drained of colour, evident in the 'white' sun and 'gray' leaves. The poet even puns on 'ash' tree, which connotes the grey ash left from a fire that has burned itself out - a fitting symbol for the end of love. The lack of colour, as well as the wintry setting, implies a cold and bitter atmosphere as well as the absence of life and joy caused by the end of the relationship. However, on another level, the title could also refer to a neutral tone of voice, one characterized by the absence of any strong emotion or partial and biased opinion. While the

speaker does strive to create a cool and emotionally detached tone that focuses on observation and retrospective reflection of 'lessons that love deceives' without seeking to apportion blame or dissect the relationship, we might want to question the  degree to which he is successful at exorcising strong emotional undercurrents from the poem.

One way in which we can detect the return of repressed emotions in the poem is through its formal structure. While Hardy did not write in the free verse which characterized many of the Modernist poets of the early twentieth century, he was a master experimenter within traditional metrical and stanzaic forms, which is why today he is recognized as the forerunner of modern poetry. While the first three lines of each stanza in *Neutral Tones* follows a fairly regular rhythm of four feet that consist of either an unstressed syllable followed by a stressed (iamb) or two unstressed syllables followed by a stressed (anapaest), such as 'We stood I by a pond I that win I ter day', the final line of each stanza disrupts the pattern and rhythm by reducing the line to just three feet, as in 'They had fallen | from an ash | and were gray'. The effect is to create an absence, the disappointment of something expected but not realized and an inarticulate longing for something unfulfilled. The rhythm falters and stumbles on the fourth line as emotional confusion rises to the poem's surface.

Loss, pain, inertia and hopelessness are also subtly inscribed within the poem's *abba* rhyme scheme ('day…God…sod…gray'). It is a pattern that suggests the failure to move forwards, a stagnation which returns to its point of origin. For Hardy's contemporary readers, this scheme was synonymous with Tennyson's monumental elegy for lost love, *In Memoriam*, which immortalized the lines 'Tis better to have loved and lost/ Than never to have loved at all'. Hardy rewrites Tennyson's elegy in lyric form. But, whereas Tennyson searched for meaning and consolation when love died, Hardy's poem focuses on emptiness, disappointment and the absence of meaning.

The final stanza accentuates the rhyme scheme's sense of inexorable entrapment and things not moving forward. Although we finally move from the past memory of the broken relationship in the first three stanzas to the reflective present of the fourth stanza, the recurring imagery of the tree and the pond, the 'God curst sun' and 'grayish leaves' returns us straight back to the first stanza in an infinite loop we cannot break out of. The use of polysyndeton and anaphora in the repeated use of 'And' at the start of sentences are further structural techniques emphasising the desire to move forward and break free coupled with the monotonous failure to do so.

Chidden of God
Another striking feature of the poem is the repeated diction and imagery of

death that permeates its lines. As well as the winter-time setting, the decaying leaves and the apocalyptic white sun, the 'starving sod' of the first stanza personifies the earth as a victim of famine and drought, the alliterative sibilance creating a harsh and even sinister effect. Often in poetry water serves as a symbol of life and vitality, but the pond setting of this poem suggests that life has stagnated and no longer flows anywhere. In Arthurian legend, the bareness of the land indicated a curse upon it as a result of an ineffectual and powerless king. Hardy's narrator is equally powerless and the undertones of a universe cosmically blighted and cursed is made explicit in references in the first and fourth stanza to the sun 'chidden of God'. The speaker of the poem exists in a universe that God has cursed by absenting himself, leaving an existence of suffering without meaning or purpose.

However, although the poem takes us to the frontiers of metaphysical speculation, this is not the main preoccupation of the poem. Rather, at the centre of the poem lies the memory of the failed relationship and, in particular, the image of the lover's face that haunts the speaker in the middle two stanzas. Eyes and lips are common images in love poetry but here, Hardy subverts their associations by making them accusatory of weariness and disillusion as with the 'eyes that rove/ Over tedious riddles' and the 'grin of bitterness'. In particular, the verb 'rove' suggests eyes that are now interested in something or someone else other. Here, the undercurrent of feeling which the title of the poem denies once again resurfaces.

The death imagery is also continued when the speaker recalls how 'The smile on your mouth was the deadest thing/ Alive enough to have strength to die.' This strange and oxymoronic description, where the superlative 'deadest' relates to something alive enough to die, suggests the lover's insincerity, but also the speaker's confused and hurt state of mind. The 'ominous bird' further indicates the expectation and portent of something dreadful to come and we realise this is the moment the speaker comprehends that love is not everlasting, something which will colour all future relationships. The

 alliterative 'wrings with wrongs' not only creates the sound of an agonized and tormented fissure in the poem, but also puns on the word 'ring' which ironically suggests a wedding ring- that symbol of immortalized love - as well as a circle in which the speaker has become ensnared; he cannot escape

from the repercussions and implication of this first realization. Where this feeling cannot be articulated, it is heard through the painful sounds of the poem, such as the 'oh' that rises from the assonantal 'rove' and 'Over' and the rhyme of 'ago' and 'fro' in the second stanza, or the tormented 'ee' sounds of the final stanza in 'keen', 'deceives', 'tree' and 'leaves'. 'Keen' also means sharp which again reveals the sense of pain that underlies the poem. Throughout the poem then, where the neutral tones of the surface suggest detachment and cool contemplation, the true, painful and inexpressible feelings frequently rise from the depths to be detected in the poem's structures, textures and sounds.

Neutral Tones crunched:

WINTER – WHITE – STARVING – ASH – EYES – TEDIOUS – WORDS – LOST – DEADEST – ENOUGH – BITTERNESS – OMINOUS – DECEIVES – WRONG – CURST – GREYISH

Robert Browning, *My Last Duchess*

Can you recognise a monster when you see one? Why of course you can; it's an essential life skill. Monsters are huge and hairy with horrible warts on their faces; they have horns on their heads and terrible claws and mouths full of spikey teeth. Monsters have wings or scales and they hiss or growl, slobber or roar, and they slither around or they scuttle, crawl or lope. Basically, monsters are amalgams of all the features we find frightening or disgusting in the animal kingdom. In short, monsters always look something like the grumpy looking little critter on our right of this page:

Right?
Wrong.

And we know where to find monsters too: In horror films and fairy tales, in the middle of the woods, under our beds, hiding in our cupboards, in nightmares.

Right?

Wrong.

Because make no mistake about it, though he's a Duke and fabulously wealthy and lives in a fabulous mansion, though he's highly refined and speaks impressively and fluently, though he is a connoisseur of fine art and is exactingly polite, even though we find him here in the elegant frame of this poem, this character is a monster. And monsters who disguise their monstrosity under an attractive façade are the most scary and dangerous monsters, right? Right.

Browning's poem is a superlative example of a dramatic monologue, a poem written in the voice of a character. As the name implies, a dramatic monologue is like a single speech from a play. A successful dramatic monologue will not only allow an insight into the character speaking but also suggest a wider narrative of which they are part. A key technique in a dramatic monologue is irony. The irony operates in the gap between what the speaking character is telling us and what the writer is telling us about them. In Browning's poem, we have several characters - the Duke, the Duchess, the Count's messenger as well as the implied voice of the poet himself. The reader is placed in the position of the messenger to whom our narrator, the Duke, tells us a story about his dead wife.

What makes this poem superlative? Think for a moment of the technical challenge Browning has set himself. Creating the authentic voice of the Duke would be a stiff challenge for any novelist, using prose, but Browning has got to make this voice sound natural and convincing whilst stringing it across a regular metre. More than that, he has also chosen to use the couplet form, a form which inevitably draws attention to the rhyme words. Notice how

Browning arranges sentences to subdue these rhymes and you'll be on your way to appreciating the Shakespearesque skill the poet employs here. And, having mentioned the bard, one way of thinking of the Duke is as kin to Shakespeare's duplicitous villains, Iago and Claudius might spring to mind. To appreciate Browning's technical accomplishment how about writing a reply to his poem in the form of a dramatic monologue in the voice of either the Count, the Duchess or the messenger?

Never stoop

The Duke is holding court. The eloquence of his words expresses his refined aristocratic manner. A domineering character, it seems he has total control of the narrative, speaking uninterrupted for 28 couplets. From the outset, he is in command, talking at, not with, the Count's messenger, politely condescending to him. Look, for example, at how he controls the topic of conversation, or how when he asks questions he doesn't wait for or allow a reply. Showing off his house and its possessions to indicate his power, prestige and wealth, the Duke establishes his credentials as a potential husband for the Count's daughter. The references to the artists, Fra Pandolf and Claus of Innsbruck, establish his cultural credentials, but also subtly contribute to the power-play. We do not know these artists and hence we are made to feel ignorant and inferior to the knowledgeable Duke. Extraordinarily self-assured, he high-handedly assumes that we, the listening audience, agree with his opinions. He portrays himself as a connoisseur of the arts and of good breeding. Indicating that he does not tolerate those who displease him, inadvertently, however, he reveals other, much darker aspects of his character. In this crucial way, Browning exerts control over the Duke.

We learn key things about the Duke's character:

- He is obsessed with control and possession
- He is extremely proud of his family heritage 'a nine-hundred years-old name'
- He has an exacting, refined sense of good taste 'here you miss / Or there you exceed the mark'
- He is breath-takingly arrogant, 'and I choose/never to stoop' (i.e. lower himself to explain how the Duchess's behaviour offended his sensibilities and pride)
- Crucially we also learn that he was murderously possessive and pathologically jealous: 'Since none puts by/ the curtain I have drawn for you, but I'.

Evil can come dressed in fine clothes, hidden by handsome manners. Slowly we come to realise that the accomplished, authoritative, intimidating manner of the Duke hides a monstrous nature: In truth, the Duke is a cruel, vindictive, merciless man. His perverse value system raises etiquette and social snobbery above morality. Specifically, he is a man who has had his wife  murdered because she was too innocent, too friendly and kind-hearted: 'I gave commands/ Then all smiles stopped together'. And now he is turning his attention to a new potential wife who he refers to chillingly as his 'object'.

One of the most horrific aspects of the Duke's aristocratic hauteur is his refusal even to tell his dead wife how her actions so offended him. He denies her even the chance to amend her ways and so avoid her doom. He doesn't even tell her what he condemns her to death for. This is made even worse, if possible, by the fact that he refuses to inform her of what 'disgusts' him, simply because he regards this as beneath his dignity, 'I choose/ never to stoop'. It is chilling too how the Duke shows no remorse. And there is also no suggestion that he will, or could, be brought to justice for murder. Because he is a Duke he seems to be above and beyond the law. He could do with his wife as he liked because of who he was and the warped values of the society in which he lived.

The cultured impression we form of the Duke is generated by the language he uses and how he uses it. In addition to using complex vocabulary what is most striking is the Duke's syntax and sentence construction. Scan the poem quickly and you'll notice there are lots of hyphens, question marks and semi-colons. In themselves, these punctuation marks suggest linguistic complexity and this is enhanced by the construction of the Duke's sentences. The longest run over nine lines, moving forward, but also halting frequently, with many clauses and parentheses, giving the impression that the fastidious Duke is trying to be very precise and exact about what he is saying. There's something sinuous to how these long sentences uncoil across lines. In stark contrast the key lines in the poem are much shorter and blunter: 'This grew; I gave commands/ Then all smiles stopped together'.

The Duke's linguistic command is also conveyed metrically. In Renaissance literature, nobility of language is often taken to express nobility of character. A regular rhythm conveys poise and control over language. Here the language moves easily and fluently forward with the character speaking the lines fully in charge of what he is saying. Here is refined and elegant articulacy. A regular pattern also gives the poet something from which to deviate. In these deviations lies significance.

Look at the section from line 29 – 43, for instance, and you will see that the pattern of the verse becomes a little less smooth and regular. Browning achieves this by extensive use of caesura and hyphens. Line 31, for instance, contains multiple pauses, small hesitations and breaks in the flow: two beats then a comma, two more, then a full stop, three more beats followed by a comma and a hyphen, one beat and an exclamation mark. The disruption is enhanced by syntax that is contorted: The clause 'I know not how' is awkwardly stuck in the middle of the sentence and the exclamatory 'good' is suddenly interjected:

'…Or blush, at least. She thanked men, - good! but thanked…'

Despite the best efforts of our will, our body language often gives away what we are really feeling. Similarly, slips in the metrical pattern betray the Duke's uncharacteristic discomposure here, the difficulty he is having maintaining his facade. Simultaneously such metrical irregularities bring these crucial lines to our closer attention.

A heart too soon made glad

Her husband describes her in a way intended to make the listener unsympathetic to the Duchess. From the Duke's haughty point of view, she was far too free with her favour, just too friendly. But these qualities viewed negatively by the Duke may well be read as positive attributes, especially by

modern readers. For example, the Duchess is shown to have an intense emotional quality: 'the depth and passion' of an 'earnest glance', and a ready capacity for happiness, 'twas not/ her husband's presence only, called that spot/ of joy into the Duchess' cheek', she had a 'heart...too soon made glad'. She seems generous spirited, tending to 'like whate'er/ she looked on' and she is appreciative and courteous, 'she thanked men'. Whereas the Duke condemns her lack of discernment; the reader warms to her lack of snobbery and prejudice, her appreciation of simple, ordinary things: 'the dropping of the daylight...the white mule...all and each/ would draw from her alike the approving speech'. The Duke suggests that there may have been something flirtatious in her manner: 'her looks went everywhere'; we infer this perception is infected by his acute jealousy. 'Her looks went everywhere' may mean simple that she smiled at everyone.

What the Duke really cannot bear is her lack of appreciation for his aristocratic lineage: She seemed to weigh 'my gift of a nine-hundred-years-old name/ with anybody's gift'. In other words, she was not socially snobbish and did not behave as if she was superior to other people. To the Duke this behavior was an unforgivable insult to his pride and honour. So, we can conclude that the Duke is haughty, emotionally and morally cold, as well as being supremely arrogant; the Duchess is his opposite; warm, vivacious, appreciative, charming. And for that he has her killed.

The painting of the Duchess is particularly significant. It reveals qualities of the central characters: the vivacity of the Duchess and the contrasting cold psychotic jealousy of her husband. Why is the Duke happier with the copy of the Duchess than with the real thing? Because he can control access to the painting, and because in it the Duchess is static, passive, unchanging. He views the painting and the person as possessions, the former adds to his status and esteem; alive, the Duchess detracted from it. A crucial detail is that 'Her mantle laps/ over my lady's wrist too much'. Like costumes in the theatre, dress in Renaissance paintings is very important. The mantle is the sleeve of her costume and it is a crucial, but characteristically ambiguous symbol. It suggests that there was something about the Duchess that was transgressive, 'laps over', and perhaps excessive 'too much'. In other words, in her own small way the Duchess stepped over boundaries. Of course, this quality can be viewed positively, reflecting somebody not bound by snobbish rules and regulations, someone who does not follow convention for convention's sake. But it can also be read negatively, as revealing someone who is ill mannered, who doesn't follow the correct polite behaviour. Moreover, it implies than even the very slightest non-compliance with strict rules, exceeding in some way 'the mark', will not only be noticed and frowned upon, but also severely punished.

The voice of Browning

As we have noted, the critical device used in dramatic monologues is irony.

Irony undermines and transforms superficial meaning. And it is in the irony we hear the moral voice of the poet and his criticism of the values of society. Through picking up implied meaning, by reading between the lines, we hear Browning's voice behind the Duke's. For the Duke, addressing the messenger, his subject is his possessions, his house and especially his artworks. But, for Browning, addressing us, the readers, the subject is the Duke himself. The irony works against the Duke and in favour of the Duchess: The Duke presents himself in a way he assumes to be favourable. He assumes we will agree with his worldview, his values and his behaviour. He assumes will be impressed by his grand demeanour and style. In fact, his behaviour and his values are shown to be vile and reprehensible. What he takes to be taste, we read as snobbery; what he takes to be honour, we read as selfish egotism and pride; what he presents as good breeding, we read as cold, pathological, murderous jealousy.

A noble frame

Browning's poem is one long, solid and unbroken stanza, comprising 28 rhymed couplets. If it were a building the poem would be a palace, or perhaps an elegant and well-constructed fortress. There are no breaks, or gaps or chinks of weakness in this fortress. The form of rhymed iambic couplets Browning employs is sometimes called heroic verse, a form that constitutes another part of the façade of the Duke. The elegant, noble form of heroic verse, clicking harmoniously into its repeated patterns is like expensive clothes and fine manners, hiding the fundamental monstrosity of the Duke. The poise and balance of the verse is his outer manner in action. Moreover, as Stephen Fry writes, Browning creates a 'ironic contrast between the urbane conversational manner, the psychotic darkness of the story and the elegant solidity of a noble form. The heroic verse is the frame out of which character can leap; it is itself the nobly proportioned, exquisitely tasteful palace in which ignobly misproportioned, foully tasteless deeds are done'.[3]

My Last Duchess crunched:
DUCHESS – ALIVE – WONDER – STANDS – LOOK – DESIGN –
STRANGERS – EARNEST – NONE – I – SEEMED – HOW – SIR –
HUSBAND'S – JOY – LAPS – TOO – FAINT – DIES –
THOUGHT – JOY – HEART – EASILY – EVERYWHERE – MY –
DROPPING – FOOL – MULE – ALL – APPROVING – THANKED
– RANKED – GIFT – ANYBODY'S – TRIFLING – WILL – JUST –
DISGUSTS – EXCEED – LESSONED – EXCUSE – STOOPING –
NEVER – WITHOUT – COMMANDS – STOPPED – ALIVE –
REPEAT – MASTER'S – PRETENSE – DOWRY – DAUGHTER'S –
OBJECT – NEPTUNE – TAMING – ME

NB
Despite the hostility of her domineering father, in 1846 Robert Browning secretly courted and married Elizabeth Barrett. A few days later the two poets escaped family and society outrage by eloping to Italy. Their shocking behaviour was condemned stridently by Elizabeth's father, who disinherited her, and by her brothers. Six years older than Robert, Elizabeth had been a recluse and was disabled; hence she did fit the convention of the perfect wife. Though Browning's poem features Renaissance characters, it is simultaneously about Victorian society and powerfully expresses a growing awareness of, and protest against, the abuse of women by patriarchal society.

---

[3] *The Ode Less Travelled*, p.206

Elizabeth Barrett Browning, *Sonnet 43*

A modest disguise

Elizabeth Barrett Browning wrote *Sonnet 43* as a private expression of her love for fellow poet Robert Browning, with whom she had begun a secret courtship. The couple later married, but her wealthy father disowned her as he did not approve of her choice. It was only after they eloped and were married that Elizabeth mentioned she had written a series of sonnets about her husband while they were courting. When Robert read them, he thought they were the best sonnets written in English since Shakespeare's and encouraged her to publish. However, they were so personal and revealing, having never been intended for anyone other than Elizabeth Barrett Browning herself, that they were published under the title *Sonnets from the Portuguese*, in an attempt to pretend they were obscure translations of another poet, rather than intimate expressions of her own private emotions. Some of the sonnets, such as *Sonnet 29*, are intensely personal and express a love that is passionate and erotic. *Sonnet 43*, in contrast, conveys a more spiritual, devotional and platonic sort of love. Nevertheless, the reader is given unusually intimate access to the poet's private feelings.

Breadth and depth and height

The short opening question immediately creates a sense of a private conversation, as if the poet is responding to this question. The language is noticeably very simple. In the first line all the words are common monosyllables and they are employed in a literal way within two short sentences that have straightforward syntax. Such simplicity is testament to the honesty and truth of what the poet is saying; there is no need for her to dress up, inflate, disguise or aggrandise her feelings through metaphor or symbolism. Her language is direct, unvarnished and transparent.

In the following lines, however, similarly simple words are used in a more complex, figurative way. Barrett Browning employs a spatial metaphor for the soul and imagines the furthest limits it could stretch - to its utmost 'depth and

 breadth and height'. Such is the love she feels that it fills her whole soul, reaches even into unknown dimensions ['feelings out of sight'], to furthermost extent of her 'being' and echoes the very best of herself, 'ideal grace'. And this is a poem very much of the soul; the heart, that traditional symbol of love, does not even get a mention. Instead the poem expresses a spiritual, disembodied, idealised love. Hence the religious touchstones of 'grace', 'faith', 'saints' and 'God'.

If this seems impossibly idealistic, rarefied and saintly, Barrett Browning strikes a less elevated note in the following lines. Bringing the poem down to a more ordinary pitch, she refers to the everyday and to what we 'need'. The superlative implies, however, that this not mere clamorous cravings oo desire, but rather the deepest, spiritual needs. The upright, good and virtuous aspect of this love is then developed. The poet associates her love with the universal progressive fight for justice, and praises its resistance to the allurements of ego and vanity. At this point in the poem we have reached the end of the opening eight lines, or octave. Barrett Browning's sonnet follows the Petrarchan form with a rhyme scheme of ABBA ABBA CDC DCD. Technically this is a particularly difficult version of the sonnet to handle in English because the whole construct has only four rhyme sounds, ABCD. Shakespeare's version of the sonnet, in contrast, almost doubled the number of rhyme

sounds to seven, making a Shakespearian sonnet considerably easier to write [though that's only in relative terms, of course]. The fact that Barrett Browning achieves this octave with such grace and apparent lack of effort – the words sound natural despite having to fit such a tight pattern, makes it correlate to the ideal love expressed. The form of the poem not only fits but expresses its meaning. However, a Petrarchan sonnet has a volta in around the ninth line, the first of the sestet. Conventionally sonnets have a call and response or question and answer structure, with the sestet [final six lines] responding to the octave. A volta marks a turn in the subject of a sonnet, sometimes signalled with a 'but' or 'however' or similar signposts for a switch in perspective.

Look for the volta in *Sonnet 43* and you'll not be able to find it. Despite expectations that they must come, no counterarguments to the propositions set out in the octave appear. Instead the poem runs straight over and continues expressing the same loving sentiments, only in new ways. The first line of the sestet, for instance, begins with exactly the same phrase, 'I love thee' as the previous two lines of the octave have done, and overall this simple phrase is repeated four times in both halves of the poem. Hence the whole the depth and breadth and height of the sonnet is filled with ideal love.

After the references to faith, grief and faith, Barrett Browning finishes her sonnet with language that is simple, unadorned and poignant:

'I love thee with the breath/ smiles, tears of all my life'

Moreover, such a love, she tells us, will not only transcend death and become immortal: Perfect though it already is, it will also be refined by death.

The danger with such a restrained and graceful expression of such an elevated, ideal love is that it will feel overly chaste and bloodless; it may seem a love more suitable for angels than for human beings. Though there is a reference to 'passion', this is not the fiery or dangerous passions of erotic or sensual love. Rather it is passion in terms of strong and earnest feelings. There is also a little sense of excited agitation in the lines we quoted above, created by a run of unstressed syllables in both lines and the tripartite list. But perhaps we need to read some of the other sonnets to find the real passion in Barrett Browning's love for Robert. It is surely significant that this poem is the penultimate one in the sequence.

As readers, we are placed in the position of the beloved. We are addressed directly as 'thee' and this rather archaic, perhaps timeless, pronoun is used in almost every line. How would you feel if someone said all this to you? How might Robert have felt? Delighted? Flattered? Daunted? All of these? Perhaps you might like to write his response, in either letter or verse form:

'Dearest Lizzie,

I read your poem and I am moved beyond words can express...'

Broadly speaking, historically, sonnets were written most often by men. Frequently they were love poems, often about, and addressed to, women. Women in sonnets tended to objectified, sometimes even deified as goddesses. So the sonnet was a form in which men could show off their wit and write something seductive. Barrett Browning colonises the dominantly male poetic space of the sonnet and demonstrates that she can too handle the form. And that she can do it with just as much panache and variety as any male writer. In this sense, her sonnets can be read from a feminist persespective. Barrett Browning's sonnets equal, or indeed, surpass male artistic achievements in the form [apart from Shakespeare, of course]. In addition, her role as a sonneeter, expressing her love for a male 'object' reflects the loosening of rigid Victorian concepts of gender and the advances made by women towards the end of the age.

Sonnet 43 crunched:

HOW – LOVE – SOUL – IDEAL – EVERY – NEED – FREELY – PURELY – PASSION – FAITH – LOSE – SAINTS – GOD - BETTER

91

Wendy Cope, *1ˢᵗ Date - She and first date - He*

Best foot forward

When we present ourselves to others we like to make the best impression we possibly can. And, like all advertising, sometimes this can lead to us emphasising, perhaps even exaggerating our best qualities and just possibly down-playing or hiding less attractive aspects of our character. Think, for instance, of how you present yourself on social media, Instagram, Facebook, Twitter etc. Probably you share flattering photographs of yourself, but delete any that don't quite do your good looks justice. It's quite natural, and we all edit the version of ourselves we present to the world to some extent. Hard though it may be, imagine, for example, you're writing a lonely hearts advert for a national newspaper or a profile for a dating website. You're unlikely to write, 'pretty average looking, a little overweight, prone to laziness, addicted to my phone, getting a bit desperate'. Even if that were the truth. Another time we are especially anxious to make a good impression is on a first date.

Wendy Cope's light comic narrative poem on the perils of dating entertainingly presents the nervousness, the misunderstandings, the misreadings and misrepresentations so common in this universal experience. The poem is a double dramatic monologue; we hear two separate misreadings of the shared first date, with each character completely mistaken about the true feelings of the other. Though the poem is comic, it is also poignant. Cope uses dramatic irony so that we, the readers, know what the characters do not; that they are so very well suited to each other. Yet it seems the poem ends with them in their separate thoughts, remaining entirely unaware of their mutual attraction.

Cupid is blind

The affinity between the 'she' and the 'he' is signalled in several fairly obvious ways. First off, the titles of each half of the narrative are identical other than the 's' in the woman's half. The way the poem is set out on the page also suggests balance and harmony. Cope could have begun the man's version of the story underneath the fourth stanza; clearly she wanted this arrangement so that two halves mirror each other, almost. Both characters words are arranged into the same regular quatrains, with a xAxA rhyme scheme and a light tetrameter. Moreover, in terms of register and language features, the two voices are very similar. At times, of course, they say precisely the same words, in the same order, at the same point in their narrative. Look, for instance are the two first lines. Other examples, or words or phrases that echo each other include 'here we are', 'quite distracted by me' and slight variations, such as 'totally into this music' and 'totally lost in the music'. At other times, they express similar sentiments – she worries that she has told him something that isn't 'exactly a lie' while he frets that he has told her something 'entirely untrue'. And, of course, they have both pretended to like classical music and are now stuck at the concert. Both also assume the other is captivated by the music ['rapt' and 'lost in'] when in fact the woman is trying to think of witty things to say and the man is desperately trying not to give away the fact that he's 'besotted' with her. The fact that the similarities are so obvious to us, yet the two characters remain blind to them, is part of what makes the situation amusing.

Having said that, the voices are so alike that it might make us wonder to what extent they are gendered at all. Could we just swap the pronouns around and there wouldn't be any difference? Not quite. Another aspect that contributes to the poem's humour is that the female character has sought to make herself attractive to her date by impressing him with her intelligence and cultured taste and she desperately tries to think of 'something clever to say'. While also wanting to present himself as cultured and interesting, the man is much more interested in the fact that his date is 'very attractive'. And he's particularly drawn to her cleavage: 'Her neckline can't fail to intrigue'. His euphemistic, indirect and polite way of expressing that line indicates the man's middle-class and middle-agedness. He also talks about the traffic and uses adjectives such as 'dreadful' and 'quite' [in the sense of total]. She uses verbs like 'thrilled' and expressions such as 'I couldn't care less' and, of course, the adjective 'quite' in the same sense. Another way in which they're well matched.

Clearly these characters are types. Rather English, rather repressed English types, easily embarrassed by social faux pas, self-conscious about how other people see them, too ashamed to make fools of their selves. Would it make any difference if Cope had given them names, such as Janice and Johnny?

Yes, because as just 'she' and 'he' they are everyman figures, versions of all of us in these sorts of awkward situations.

At the start of each half of the poem Cope employs the past tense, 'said', 'wasn't', 'hoped', 'get' and so forth. This could lead us into supposing the two characters are reporting back on their first date at some interval after it has happened. However, in both narratives, the tense switches to the present tense in the second stanzas at the concert, 'here we are'. From this point onwards the dominant tense is the present – 'I'm trying', 'I glance', 'we haven't', 'she is', but Cope also slips in a future tense each – 'I'll have'. Hence the poem ends during the concert and holds out the possibility that the two characters might eventually realise their perfect compatibility. And, in the end, don't we want them to bridge the divide of silence and space between them and find each other, soppy so-and-sos that we are. Maybe this is because we're all hopeless romantics, but maybe too because there's something winning and sympathetic about these two characters. Yes, they may be a little awkward and self-conscious and a bit foolish, but they're also modest and self-deprecating and keen to make a good impression and need to be liked. Both imagine, wrongly, that the other is not interested in them. Both underestimate themselves. More than that, don't they deserve each other?

1st Date crunched:

SAID – LIE – HOPED – HIGH – CLASSICAL – BACH – CONCERT – HALF-DARK – THRILLED – LESS – HARDEST – CLEVER – GLANCE

– RAPT – INTO – UNDISTRACTED

SAID – IMPLIED – DON'T – UNTRUE – CONCERT – DATE –
DREADFUL – LATE – TALKING – NERVOUS – LOST –
UNDISTRACTED – ATTRACTIVE – NECKLINE – BESOTTED –
LEAGUE – GLANCE – START – SAY

Carol Ann Duffy, *Valentine*

Tell me the truth about love

Right from the very first word, the negative 'no' in her first abrupt, truncated sentence Duffy makes it clear hers isn't going to be any kind of conventional love poem. This poet is not going to employ conventional symbols of love, nor offer these tired, old objects as her Valentine's gift: 'Not a red rose or a satin heart'. The first symbol was most famously used by Robert Burns in his lovely love poem 'Oh my love's like a red, red rose'. Within the first four words of Duffy's she has dismissed this symbol and all it connotes about the nature of love. Instead she's going to give her beloved an 'onion'. And Duffy might be the first poet or person who's ever lived who thinks that love is like what Wikipedia defines as a 'swollen edible bulb used as a vegetable'.

Certainly an onion seems an unlikely symbol for love and Duffy sticks full stops at the end of each of the first two lines to emphasise the comic surprise of this object. Certainly it would be hard not to be a tad disappointed by this inexpensive and distinctly unromantic gift if you were the 'you' in the poem. What would be a less romantic gift? A pair of socks? A saucepan? A revision book, perhaps on poetry? An onion has got to be right up there with the world's worst possible valentine gifts.

In the rest of the poem, Duffy develops the comparison between a loving relationship and an onion. This sort of extended metaphor is technically known as a conceit. A famous example runs through Shakespeare's sonnet 18, whose title 'Shall I compare thee to a Summer's day' rather gives away the nature of the conceit. Conceits are particularly associated with Renaissance writers and especially with a group of poets now known rather grandly as The Metaphysicals. Typically, Metaphysical poets used conceit to demonstrate their poetic wit; the more unlikely the things being compared the greater the wit required to show how they are actually rather alike. The leading Metaphysical poet, John Donne, for instance, in a move even less romantic than Duffy's, compared love to a flea. Yes, a flea. And he employed it in order to try to seduce his beloved. Yes, a flea. And that highlights another way in which Duffy boldly defies convention. She employs a device, a conceit, used extensively by male poets and used by those male poets to seduce female subjects. In Duffy's poem, however, the conceit is not used rhetorically to seduce. Instead it serves as a corrective to clichéd, soppy ideas of love; her onion offers the sharp tang of realism. As she says, though it might be less romantic, and though perhaps her partner expresses some reluctance accepting the message, Duffy has taken off the rose-tinted spectacles of Valentine's Day, and is 'trying to be truthful', about their relationship and about all relationships and about the nature of love.

So Duffy rejects conventional symbols, chooses an unconventional one and uses a conceit, but in an unconventional way. And the form of her poem is also unconventional. What's the most conventional form for a love poem? We've already mentioned it; of course it's a limerick. I mean a sonnet, like Barrett Browning's. Duffy's poem is nothing like a sonnet, in fact it's nothing like any conventional closed or open form of poem because it's written in free verse and is highly irregular. This means that the lines and stanzas and rhythm and rhyme don't follow any pre-set pattern; instead they follow their own unique, idiosyncratic impulses. This is another way in which Duffy implies her love, and love itself, is not regular, does not fit convention, is complex and difficult and unpredictable.

Look at the poem on the page and looks rather slight and delicate, maybe even fragile. The lines move in a careful, perhaps even hesitant fashion. There are lots of stops and starts, full stops and short sentence fragments, such as 'take it' and 'lethal'. These help control the delivery of the poem and convey a sense of drama - a speaking voice, slowing down, pausing or growing animated. The poem may look a little fragile and skeletal, however, if so, it's a skeleton of steel.

Love is like an onion

So, Ms. Duffy, tell us how exactly is love, or a relationship, like an onion? Well, it turns out they do have rather a lot of things in common. Firstly, the inside of an onion does look a bit like a moon, that eternal symbol of love in a relationship, and onion flesh is white, like light.  And onions also have layers, which we can 'undress'. Not only that, but onions can make us cry through their sharp, intense aroma and thus, they can distort our perceptions. Moreover, the taste of an onion is so strong it lingers on the lips and in the mouth [try kissing someone who's just eaten cheese and onion crisps, or rather don't] and on one's fingers. After chopping an onion, a knife needs washing to get rid of the clingy scent. And lastly, its rings are platinum coloured and one ring could, if shrunk, serve as a very poor excuse of a wedding-ring. So, despite seeming unlikely, an onion is shown to be an appropriate analogy for a relationship.

We might be persuaded by Duffy's wit. But it seems her addressee needs plenty of convincing. In the second line of the poem the poet passes over the gift. And she does so again four lines later in the opening word of the second stanza, after which there is a long pause. And then she explains again how she has not bought a clichéd present, this time round a 'cute-card or a kissogram' and again tries to give the beloved the 'onion'. Repetition of exactly the same line, 'I give you an onion' suggests no progress has been made, despite the poet's best efforts. We're back where we started. By the penultimate stanza the gift still hasn't been accepted. Is there a touch or annoyance in the shift to the imperative? Again a very short line, just two simple monosyllables finishes with an emphatic full stop and then a long blank line that suggests silence. As if the recipient is still considering it. Through such means Duffy helps us picture a little scene, a short piece of domestic drama, featuring repeated offer and repeated refusal. Certainly the addressee needs a bit more of a nudge, because in the next line the poet makes a rather half-hearted seeming marriage proposal: 'a wedding-ring/ if you like'. Rather ominously, straight afterward this, as if the beloved has finally accepted the gift comes the single word 'Lethal' and more portentous silence.

Why did the addressee needs so much convincing? We said at the start that Duffy's poem tries to correct overly sickly and sentimental presentations of love and relationships; that the poem was a stiff dose of oniony realism. But the poet is also persuasive, just in a different way to those lusty Metaphysicals. The poet tries to persuade their lover about the true nature of their relationship. And it's not all sweetness and light.

Valentine crunched:

ROSE – ONION – MOON – PROMISES – UNDRESSING – HERE – TEARS – LOVER – REFLECTION – GRIEF – TRUTHFUL – CUTE – ONION – FIERCE – POSSESSIVE – WE – LONG – TAKE – WEDDING-RING – IF – LETHAL – CLING - KNIFE

We mentioned earlier that it'd be hard to imagine a less Romantic symbol of love or Valentine's gift than an onion and suggested a few terrible alternatives. How about writing a version of *Valentine* replacing Duffy's onion with your own idea for the world's least romantic gift? We're so ashamed by our own version that we're going to hide it somewhere at the back of this book. But we're 100% confident you'll be able to produce something better...

Elizabeth Jennings, *One Flesh*

What happens to couples whose relationship seems to have grown tired and stale? They might decide to cut their losses and call it a day; they might make a superhuman effort to put right whatever's wrong in their relationship and end up much happier as a result. Or they might end up like the couple Elizabeth Jennings describes in *One Flesh* – a poem whose opening words, 'Lying apart', echo those of Philip Larkin in his poem *Lying in Bed*. [Jennings and Larkin knew each other at Oxford; her obituary in the Daily Telegraph notes that they used to listen to jazz records together and they are often bracketed together as Movement poets]. In this poem, Jennings describes an elderly couple whose marriage has settled over the years into a state of silent coexistence, the passion of early married life washed away by time. It's only at the end of the poem that Jennings reveals, devastatingly, that the people she describes are actually her own parents.

Not unity, but distance

The poem takes its title from a verse in Chapter Two of the Book of Genesis. We are told of the creation of Adam, from a handful of dust, and then of Eve, from one of Adam's ribs. The union of Adam with Eve – who Adam describes as 'bone from my bone, and flesh from my flesh' – is established as the model for marriage, in which 'a man leaves his father and mother and is united to his wife, and they become one flesh'. Yet right from the start of the poem, what marks out the couple in *One Flesh* is not unity, but distance. They are 'Lying apart now, each in a separate bed', and are engaged in their own different pursuits. Initially, this could appear peaceful and restful: 'He with a book, keeping the light on late, / She like a girl dreaming of childhood'. However, there's an underlying awkwardness there. His book is unread, while she is only 'like a girl' – she is actually staring at the ceiling, 'her eyes fixed on the shadows overhead'. They lie as if awaiting 'some new event', but it's not clear at this point what this might be. [By the end of the poem, we suspect that this 'new event' might actually be death – the final experience this couple must confront].

The poem's second stanza builds on this sense of uneasiness. A telling simile captures how the couple are 'tossed up like flotsam from a former passion' – like the wreckage of a ship, floating on the sea of life. Yet this is clearly not a stormy relationship. Look at 'how cool they lie'. There's a multitude of meanings packed into this simple seeming line, all of them carefully balanced against each other: 'Cool' can mean casual, or lacking heat – and this lack of heat can itself be comfortable, refreshing, or chilling and indifferent. And 'lie', of course, can refer to their physical position – or to a lack of truth. Their separateness is reiterated, very simply, in the words 'They hardly ever touch', but then this is qualified by a very telling afterthought: 'Or if they do, it is like a confession / Of having little feeling – or too much'. Whatever it is that the couple still feel for each other – love, affection, resentment, frustration, indifference – they certainly do not know how to express it. Instead, what faces them is 'chastity' – a lack of physical intimacy, an absence of sex, and the 'destination / For which their whole lives were a preparation'. It's a pretty bleak prospect.

The Poetry Archive website praises Jennings' work for its 'emotional restraint' and 'unassuming technical craft'. The former is certainly in evidence in *One Flesh*, but it's interesting to see how much it depends on the latter. The first stanza consists of one long sentence, but it's a sentence that begins with a build-up of adjectival and noun phrases that we must make our way through before we get to the main active verb, 'is', in the second half of the fourth line. And even when we get to this main verb, it's immediately postmodified by 'as if'. The overall effect is of stasis – the couple are frozen, as if in a photograph. In turn this creates unease as we anticipate some sort of development – mirroring, of course, the couple lying in their separate beds as if awaiting 'some new event'. There are long, mournful vowel sounds in 'late', 'light', 'like' and 'wait', a predominance of soft consonants such as 'l' and 'w' and 's', and an ABABAA rhyming pattern in the first two stanzas in which the first and third lines are half-rhymes – establishing, very quickly, a sense of quiet dissatisfaction. In the second stanza, the rhyming words in the A lines – 'passion', 'confession', 'destination' and 'preparation' are what's known as feminine rhymes, words where the stresses fall on the penultimate syllable, leaving the rhyming syllables unstressed. It's a fitting technique to use in a poem about a relationship that hasn't been blown apart, but has simply slid into complacency. Notably the B rhymes are, of course, all masculine. Neatly on a structural level this rhyme scheme first separates As and Bs and then brings them together in a couplet at the end of each stanza, suggesting a deeper connection between the two characters than their surface separation implied.

In the final stanza, the rhyming pattern changes to ABABAB, a subtle shift that gives a sense of reaching some kind of development and perhaps resolution. It begins with a line that sums up this couple's relationship, united by time and habit but seemingly not much else: they are 'strangely apart, yet strangely close together'. The silence between them is described in a simile – 'like a thread to hold / And not wind in' – which suggests that they are aware of the distance between them but unwilling [or unable?] to do anything to break it. The metaphor that follows this – 'And time itself's a feather, /Touching them gently' – underscores the sense of a relationship that is being gradually eroded by the passing of the years, in a way that's barely noticed. The delicate images Jennings uses – holding a thread, being touched by a feather – could be seen as a sign that there is still some tenderness left in this marriage. For whatever reason, however, the couple is unable to access it.

The poem ends with a question, and it's only in this final sentence that the narrator reveals that the couple are her mother and father. The passion that once existed between them – the 'fire from which I came' – has died down, 'grown cold', and they have become old almost without noticing the passing of the years. There's a sense that Jennings [who was 40 when this poem was published] is questioning not only whether her parents recognise what has happened to their marriage, but also what this means for her, looking at them from the vantage point of her own adulthood. But the poem doesn't push this train of thought any further: instead, it leaves it as a possibility, in its characteristically observant but unobtrusive manner.

Not distance, but unity?

Of course, there's another possible interpretation, supported by the rhyme scheme and some of Jennings' choices of phrase: Perhaps the couple are so close that they don't need to demonstrate this closeness – they are happy to give each other 'their own space', to sink into companionable silences. See, for instance, how the mirroring phrase 'strangely apart, yet strangely close' both separates and links them. Or consider how many times Jennings uses the plural pronouns, 'they', 'their' and 'them'. The couple is seen entirely through the eyes of Jennings-as-narrator, and this gives her a power to depict their relationship in whatever way she chooses, presenting them through her own particular filter. Maybe she has misinterpreted the feelings her parents had for each other; maybe, given a right of reply, they'd tell a very different story. But all of this is outside the text, and the words on the page are all we have to go on – words that quietly but firmly point out the ironies in the poem's title.

One Flesh crushed:

APART – LATE – DREAMING – WAIT – NEW – SHADOWS – FLOTSAM – COOL – CONFESSION – FEELING – CHASTITY – WHOLE – STRANGELY – SILENCE – TIME – GENTLY – TWO – COLD

John Cooper Clarke, *I wanna be yours*

The Saltford Sinatra

Set the students the task of writing a love poem using all the objects on the next page. There's a Ford Cortina, the Atlantic Ocean, a raincoat, an electric meter and an electric heater, a teddy bear, a coffee pot and a vacuum cleaner. Give them ten teacher minutes. Once they've had a good go at this, you might take pity on them and add a few more words to help things along. If you're feeling particularly generous you might tell them that the following words all come at the end of lines:

Dust, rust, dreamboat, sail away, anywhere, out, lotion, devotion, emotion.

Once they've sweated over that for as long as you deem sufficient, you can give them the first line of the poem and, perhaps even, a few others. Their task then is to try to complete the poem:

Let me be your Ford Cortina   Let me be your vacuum cleaner

Let me your dreamboat	Take me with you anywhere
I will not run out	That's how deep is my ocean

Alternatively, if this sounds too complicated or demanding, just give them the first stanza and ask them to complete the poem. Once they've read the actual poem, challenge them to write an extra or alternative stanza in the same inimical 'Saltford Sinatra' style.

Machine gun verse

Big spikey-haired, drain-pipe trousered punk performance poet, dj, social and cultural commentator, rock star, TV personality and comic wit, John

Cooper Clarke, is renowned for the rapid-fire delivery of his often blisteringly caustic poems. Check out the Mancunian motormouth on YouTube and you'll find plenty of choice examples. But, be warned, especially if you have a sensitive disposition, Clarke's machine gun poetry takes no prisoners and his language can be what's somewhat euphemistically called earthy and forthright.

I wanna be yours has been set to music by The Artic Monkeys, a fact that highlights the poem's sonorous qualities. In particular, the poem obviously features a lot of repetition of words and phrases. The title phrase pops up in over a third of the lines and the adjective 'deep' appears ten times. In fact, there's a whole line composed of this single adjective, repeated six times to sound like a chorus in an old-fashioned rock and roll song. The repetitive patterning is enhanced by a rhyme scheme that bolts together paired rhymes with a triple rhyme for two stanzas and with a quadruple rhyme in the last stanza. So, there's a lot of rhyme for a short poem. And full rhymes are used, generating an emphatic sonic repetition. The poem's swing and sense of momentum is generated mostly, however, by Clarke's use of metre.

As with the rhyme scheme, the metrical pattern of the first half of each stanza is distinct from the second. The quatrains follow a ballad form of cross-rhymed lines alternating between tetrameter and trimeter. The stressed syllables are indicated below by an oblique back slash, the unstressed by crosses:

x /   x /   x   / x   /   x
I **wan** na **be** your **vac** uum **clean** er

/   x / x   /
Breath ing **in** your **dust**

The combination of the metre and the rhyme set the poem off at a fair lick. Two lines of rhymed tetrameter come next, followed by a snappy two beat line, 'you **call** the **shots**' creating a sense of shortening, speeding up and intensifying. The choice of the words adds to the sense of speed and bouncy emphatic quality of the verse. Consider, for example, what difference there'd be if the poem started with 'I want to be your'. As well as sounding more like ordinary, vernacular speech, 'wanna' sets the poem running at a nifty speed as the sounds of its opening words run into each other.

Neatly the form of the poem incorporates patterns of twos and threes and forges hybrid stanza forms. For example, as we've seen, two types of different quatrains are fused into each of its stanzas. These stanzas also feature pairs and triple rhymes as well as a double pair in the last stanza. And, of course, there are three stanzas, two of which follow the same rhyme pattern and a final one that switches the three rhymes to four. Clearly these patterns are relevant to the major theme of a poem that attempts to persuade a woman to become a man's partner and which, in its final stanza, introduces a potential spanner into the works - a possible third party in the relationship. 'I don't want to be **hers**'.

The voice behind the haircut

As well as the song-like qualities of the lexical and syntactical repetition, the metre and the rhymes, another pop characteristic of Clarke's poem is his use

of mundane, everyday objects. Conventionally in poetry love is expressed through elaborate and flattering comparisons. A lover might expect to be compared with romantic motifs, such as the sun or the moon or a summer's day, 'more lovely and more temperate' as Shakespeare wrote. And ardent lovers seeking to seduce a beloved tend to compare themselves to things rare and precious. It's less conventional to compare oneself to a Ford Cortina.

It's good practice to have a go at any writing tasks we set a class — if we can't/won't do it, it'd be a bit rich to expect our students to. In that spirit, we had a go at the creative writing task suggested at the start of this essay and came up with the following.

I wanna be your Maserati,
Very sleek and fast,
I wanna be your birthday party
We will have a blast.
If you like your champagne brut
Let me be your champagne flute,
Admit, it, I'm kinda cute,
I wanna be yours.

Whatever you think of the quality of our effort, it should help highlight the self-deprecating, comic quality of Clarke's self-imagining. A Ford Cortina, for instance, was a common, solidly mid-market family saloon. It's hardly a racy, rare or exciting car, like a Maserati or a Ferrari. Nor could you 'pimp up' a Cortina to make it look cool. Basically, it was a pretty boring, ordinary car. What the poet/car offers is reliability, not dynamism, romance or any sense of thrill — he/it will 'never rust'. Clarke also compares himself to every day household and kitchen appliances — heaters, coffee pots and vacuum cleaners, and it's hard to imagine anything much more unromantic than an electric meter or 'setting lotion'. Even the more overtly romantic images are presented in terms of their utility: he offers to be like a teddy bear but only so she can 'take him anywhere'; he describes himself as a 'dreamboat', but only in terms of being a useful escape vehicle. The normally inflated, intoxicated, hyperbolic language of love poetry is elbowed aside by images that are much more down-to-earth and homely. Combined, the series of metaphors imply Clarke will be a reliable, comforting and protecting figure. And a witty, modest, self-deprecating one to boot.

I wanna be yours crunched:

LET – YOUR – CORTINA – RUST – NOT – POT – CALL – YOURS – RAINCOAT – RAINY – DREAMBOAT – AWAY – ME – CARE – WANNA- ELECTRIC – OUT – HEATER – WITHOUT – DEVOTION – DEEP – EMOTION – DEEP – HERS - YOURS

Jen Hadfield, *Love's Dog*

Like *I wanna be yours*, Hadfield's poem lends itself well to creative approaches. Give a class the first five lines and then every other line. Having established that the poem follows a couplet form, with each line beginning with 'what I love' or 'hate' about love, the class should be able to come up with some possible lines. For example, the eighth line could be 'what I love about love is its truthful delirium' and the tenth line could be 'what I hate about love is its queasy motion'. This kind of engagement should generate some curiousity about the lines Hadfield choose and foreground the ways in which she deviates from the patterns she sets up. This should make us wonder why, for instance, the eleventh line, ends with the unromantic image of a 'boil-wash' and doesn't have a partner in rhyme or even in half-rhyme.

Obviously, if we separate the poem's lines into positives and negatives about love we can more clearly she which aspects of love the poet celebrates and which aspects she criticises. Doing this we'll likely to find that while some of the lines can be decoded fairly easily others are far more elusive. So, the positives, of which there are more than the negatives, are that:

1. Love helps us to understand ourselves or itself – it's 'diagnostic' and it's a 'truth serum'.

2. Love is generous, giving of itself without restraint – 'its Eat-me/Drink-me'. This image also implies love sustains us, is essential to existence. There's a suggestion of an erotic dimension too here, I think.

3. Love gives us great riches, 'doubloons'. [Doubloons, rather than say gold coins might also make us think of pirates, parrots and looted treasure.]

4. Love is exciting, it makes us feel giddy, it turns our world upside down; it's like being in a 'spin-cycle'. Exciting and adventurous and perhaps dangerous too, like a 'pirate'.

But what about love's 'bird-bones'? What does that convey to you about love? Maybe that love can be delicate and fragile? And how is it like a 'petting zoo'? Because it might feature a lot of stroking? And, for that matter how is the lover like a zookeeper? Perhaps because a zookeeper is in charge of all the petting animals.

On the other hand, the negative aspects of love, according to Hadfield, include:

1. It helps forecast what's going to go wrong with us; it provides a 'prognosis'

2. It's selfish to the point of egotistical obsession. 'me, me, me'.

3. It can make you, or everything other than itself, feel small and insignificant; it's a 'shrinking potion'. Love gone wrong can reduce us. The shrinking potion coupled with the labels 'Eat-me/Drink-me' allude to Lewis Carroll's

Alice in Wonderland. Whereas the first allusion expresses a positive about love, the second conveys a negative. So, even in this allusion to a novel itself full of logic puzzles Hadfield's poem is elusive and ambiguous.

Mad Hatter's tea party

Then things get a bit trickier and the poem becomes more like a puzzle without sufficient clues. Love is like a 'boil-wash', perhaps because this a harsh sort of wash, the hottest sort. If you were a piece of clothing, a 'boil-wash' would probably be rather unpleasant. 'Bonemeal' makes some sense too, as this is a mixture of ground animal bone mixed with waste products from abattoirs and is used commonly as a fertilizer. Certainly, it sounds pretty disgusting and from this disgustingness new things sprout. Why, though, is love like 'burnt toast' or a 'bent cigarette'? My guess is that burnt toast is about disappointment, distraction and waste. Maybe a 'bent cigarette' is a broken one, or one that's been smoked. And,

of course, cigarettes are horribly addictive and, in the long term, deadly. By the time we arrive at the last image, of the 'sick parrot' we're likely to be developing the distinct feeling that the poet is toying with us, toying with readers' desire to decode images by giving us a series of increasingly bizarre and impossible to solve 'clues'. Go on, Jed, we might reasonable say, exasperatedly, tell us, how is love in any way like a 'bent cigarette' or, indeed like a 'sick parrot'? Is this some kind of a joke? And, while we're about it, why is your poem called *Love's Dog* when this dog is conspicuously absent?

Perhaps that last line is a sort of joke because it seems to allude to the famous 'dead parrot' sketch by Monty Python. Or maybe love is like a parrot because lovers end up parroting what each other say, repeating each other without real understanding. Clearly Hadfield is playing around with the common phrase 'sick as a parrot', so maybe she just means that love is like a disease. Maybe. The point, though, is that the poem's teasing and playful and we can't come to definitive decodings of its images. As for the title, this is lifted from a poem by the Scottish poet Edwin Morgan called A *View of Things*, from which Hadfield also got the repetitive line structure of her poem. Interesting enough, but it doesn't really explain why she used this as the title. Perhaps the playfulness of the poem itself expresses love; perhaps this playfulness is itself like a dog. Maybe. Perhaps the poem cannot be fully decoded, because neither can love. We might think we can break it down, explain it, rationalise it, but love remains somehow mysterious.

Is love the opposite of hate? Are they the far ends, the outer poles on a continuum of emotions? Or are these two emotions more closely together than we generally like to think? Can love curl back around and become hate? Obviously Hadfield had to think of rhyme words to complete each couplet. But that didn't mean she had to use words that have such similar meanings or that come from the similar lexical fields. For instance, both 'diagnosis' and 'prognosis' are associated with medicine; the first identifies what is wrong and the second suggests what will happen to the patient as a consequence. So a diagnosis usually leads to a prognosis. Surely the poet could have thought of an alternative rhyme for 'me' than the one she chose. A 'serum' is similar to a 'potion'; when you're washing clothes you might well use either or both a 'spin-cycle' and a 'boil-wash'. Pirates often have parrots on their shoulders, at least in films they do. In contrast, the couplets that focus on just

116

love or just hate have end words that have less in common, 'zoo'/ 'you'; 'doubloons/ bird-bones'; 'bonemeal/ cigarette'.

Where's all this heading? Hadfield uses almost identical words for the first seven words of every line in her poem. All that changes in the lines is 'love' sometimes becomes 'hate' and the last word or words vary. Add to that the fact that there's no predictable pattern to when she will use 'love' and 'hate' – they don't alternate, for example – and we arrive at the idea that the poet is suggesting that these two apparently opposite emotions are actually very close together and the one can easily become the other.

Love's crunched *Dog*:
[Obviously in a poem 90% of which is composed of the same words, most of the most important words are going to be the rhyming ones at the ends of lines. But maybe that's not always the case...]

LOVE – HATE – ME – DRINK-ME – ZOO – YOU – TRUTH – SHRINKNG – DOUBLOONS – BIRD-BONES – BOIL-WASH – SPIN-CYCLE – LOATHE – BENT – PIRATE – SICK

Vernon Scannell, *Nettles*

Walking wounded

Few poets' lives have been quite as dramatic and colourful as Vernon Scannell's [1922-2007]. As a young man Scannell served in the British Army in WWII, fighting in North Africa, including in the battle of El Alamen. Disgusted by the aftermath of battle, Scannell deserted from the army and went on the run. Arrested and sentenced to three years in prison, he spent six months in 'one of the harshest penal institutions in Alexandria'[4] only securing his release by volunteering to fight in the Normandy landings. Sometime later, Scannell deserted again from the army and spent two whole years on the run. After he was captured, he was court-marshalled and sent to a military hospital for treatment. Before becoming a professional writer and broadcaster, Scannell worked as a school teacher and as a professional boxer, working for a time in a fairground boxing booth.

---

[4] https://en.wikipedia.org/wiki/Vernon_Scannell

The homefront of domesticity

Scannell's wartime experiences and what we now would call post-traumatic stress disorder lend this poem about an ordinary experience a deeper and more poignant resonance. Though the poet is describing a common domestic situation, Scannell uses a range of words, a lexical field, associated with warfare, including 'spears', 'regiment', 'blade', 'parade', 'fallen dead', 'recruits' and 'wounds'. And this military dimension to the poem helps explain the seemingly irrational and disproportionate way in which the speaker reacts to his son falling into a bed of nettles. Though he takes care of his son and 'soothed' him, the main focus of the poem is on the speaker's reaction to the incident, with almost half of the poem's lines detailing this.

In the *Oxford Companion to Modern Poetry*, the authors comment on Scannell's poetry expressing a 'resilient compassionate concern for ordinary human life' and the description of the son reflects this concern. We hear of his 'sobs and tears' and see the 'white blisters' on the 'tender skin' and eventually his 'watery grin'. However, at the start of the poem the child is introduced as 'my son', but in line five he has already become the less tender, more generic 'the boy'. This shift indicates the way the poem will move from the individual experience of an individual child to a more generalised comment on inevitability of hurt and suffering in life. The Oxford Companion authors go on to say that Scannell's 'tenderness is qualified by a kind of brusque disenchantment'.[5] Certainly *Nettles* demonstrates a mixture of compassion and stoical disaffection.

After honing his 'blade' the speaker 'went outside and slashed in fury with it' until he has destroyed every single nettle. While it might make sense to get

---

[5] The Oxford Companion to Modern Poetry, pp 547-7

rid of the nettles, the intensity of this emotional response - his 'fury' and the violence of the verb 'slashed' - is harder to explain. Why should the speaker be so enraged about a perfectly natural plant? Being stung by nettles is a perfectly ordinary experience and does no lasting harm. What's the big deal? Clearly the speaker is transferring onto the nettles feelings of rage bottled up within him. The speaker just has to get rid of this rage, somehow, and the nettles  provide an opportunity, an excuse to completely let rip. But, the military metaphors personify the nettles; they are a 'fierce parade'; he makes a 'funeral pyre' of them and even calls them the 'fallen dead'. Clearly the rage and violence the speaker feels stems from his traumatic military experience and it expresses profound hostility against the army and/or against warfare.

But it's more than this too. It seems that the poet is angry at the enduring capacity for conflict in human beings and of pain within nature. As well as the timeless reference to 'spears', the speaker's attempts to eradicate his world of the nettles and everything they symbolise about the capacity of the world to hurt us without cause, fail. Only a fortnight later, 'tall recruits' have replaced the nettles he'd cut down. This implies stubborn persistence and resistance. And the connivance of the most powerful forces in nature, those sustaining life, sunlight and water, in the endurance of this harm. Personifying nature as 'busy' adds to the sense that this harm is intended, that some metaphysical force actively intends it. With its shift in perspective, the disenchanted declarative last line of the poem seems to accept there is nothing the speaker could have done or can do to protect his son from being

120

hurt by life. The idea is presented as a statement of fact, seemingly without emotion:

'My son would often feel sharp wounds again'.

In a more general sense, the line suggests not only the son, but all humans have to face hurt and pain and suffering from life, that suffering is an inherent part of the human condition. Moreover, according to the poet, sometimes, it seems, the world and nature is actively hostile to us, cruel, malicious even. Hence Scannell describes the nettles as a 'regiment of spite'.

Harmonising the sadness of the universe

For a poem that includes destructive rage and feelings of helplessness in the face of insurmountable odds, it's arranged in a remarkably orderly way. In fact, Scannell organsises his material with almost military good order. The poem's a type of extended sonnet, comprising four quatrains each neatly cross-rhymed ABAB and so forth. Full, masculine rhymes click into place and the poem runs smoothly along lines of fairly even pentameter. There are a few ruffles in the order, however. In the first line, for example, 'fell' takes a stress, so that the third metrical foot is reversed into a trochee [stress/ unstress]. Later, an extra syllable adds a subtle sense of lost control to the tenth line. But other than those tiny irregularities, the poem's remarkably composed and controlled. In other words, the form strikes an optimistic counterbalance to the sentiments expressed in the last line. However difficult or troubling the material of the poem may be, the capacity for the artist to frame and control this is stronger. In this sense, we could argue that Scannell's poem is not, in fact, disenchanted. Indeed, we could argue that the poet successfully applies one of his own favourite comments about poetry from A.E. Housman and manages in *Nettles* to 'harmonise' the 'sadness of the universe'.

Nettles crushed:

SON – SPEARS – SPITE – SOBS – BOY – TENDER – SOOTHED – GRIN – BLADE – FURY – PARADE – UPRIGHT – DEAD – SUN – RECRUITS – AGAIN

With its subject of the inevitability of trauma in human life and imagery drawn from the military, *Nettles* could be compared to the next poem, Armitage's *The Manhunt*. Both poems are about the enduring psychological damage soldiers can suffer from their combat experiences. Both poems also mix tenderness with a more detached perspective on their subjects.

Simon Armitage, *The Manhunt*

War poetry

The most famous and celebrated war poets tend to be those who experienced combat first-hand. For unforgettable, visceral descriptions of WWI we turn to writers such as Wilfred Owen and Siegfried Sassoon. Probably the most celebrated WWII poet is Keith Douglas who, like Owen, was killed in action. The fact that these poets were first-hand witnesses to the horrors of war lends their poetry the potency of testimony. If you are a modern poet who has never been a soldier and has never fought in a battle, you might well hesitate and consider carefully before trying to write a war poem. Readers might believe that only those who have had direct experience of war are capable of describing it, and for a civilian to try this would be at best an act of crass insensitivity and at worst of opportunistic appropriation. It's not then without qualms that a poet as self-aware as Simon Armitage would choose such a difficult subject.

And by all accounts, Armitage did not only rely on the power of his own imagination. Instead he conducted many interviews with soldiers and their partners before writing poems that contributed to a moving television documentary for Channel 4 about returning war veterans, called *The Not Dead*. You can hear him talking about this process as well as a poignant reading of *The Manhunt* at: www.youtube.com/watch?v=TtDiOsQsnRw. Here the poet talks about the responsibility he felt in writing about real people's lives, 'real people who had been involved in conflicts where people had been injured and died and who have killed people as well'.

A sweating, unexploded mine

This context helps explain Armitage's decision not to write in the voice of the soldier himself. Instead he chooses to compose this dramatic monologue in the voice of a partner, perhaps the soldier's wife. What is the effect of this choice of narration? The most important one, I think, is that it results in the soldier remaining silent; we never hear his voice or his version of what happened to him. This means he remains something of a mystery to us, we only view him from the outside and through the eyes of his partner; we have

no access to his private thoughts. In this sense, he is lost to us as readers in an analogous way to how he is lost to his partner, a kind of blank we try to fill. The hunt of the title is her and, through her, our attempt to 'find' him. For some soldiers a symptom of what used to be  called shellshock was mutism and for many soldiers, in many wars, it has been difficult or impossible to talk about their traumatic experiences. Making the soldier the subject of the poem, but not its narrator, also helps to present him as an everyman figure, standing in for all damaged combatants in all wars. Hence this soldier's silence has a greater, wider, more poignant resonance.

What we do learn about him is how his body has been horribly damaged by war. The poem presents him as a series of wrecked body parts, a collection of broken pieces that have to be put together gently and carefully in order to try to reconstruct the whole person he once was. A 'frozen river' runs 'through his face'; his jaw is a 'blown hinge'; his should-blade is a 'fractured rudder'. Every fragmentary piece of him is itself also 'broken', 'grazed' or scarred. Usually comparing somebody to objects, such as hinges and rudders dehumanises them. And we would expect this to lead us to feel less sympathy - it's harder for us to care about things rather than people. But here, Armitage manages to make his metaphors have the reverse effect, generating greater sympathy. Maybe this is because they imply that the solider himself feels dehumanised, just an assemblage of mechanical bits and parts. Worse, though she is expressing tenderness towards him, it seems that his partner now also sees him in this dehumanised way.

Arguably the instances of physical damage to the outer self are less significant than the emotional and psychological damage to his inner self. Hinges can be fixed, rudders put back together, rivers can unfreeze. Nursing the inner person back to health will probably be more difficult, a fact acknowledged by the way the partner starts with the physical suffering. Slowly this allows her to work towards discovering and then dealing with the locked away and buried mental trauma. How, for instance, do you treat a 'grazed heart', a heart that has been hurt and maybe now finds it difficult to express love? How do you minister to a mind which has buried within it the capacity for explosive, annihilating destruction?

Only then

This is the difficult, delicate and perhaps dangerous task facing the poem's speaker. She describes herself as like an explorer carefully moving over potentially hostile territory in search of a clue, or first cause or 'source', something, anything that will allow them to reach the soldier mentally and emotionally and help him deal with his trauma. One hesitant step at a time, 'climbing' and 'skirting along', the narrator is allowed to 'trace' and 'explore' and 'search'. Alongside the language of exploration runs the language of nursing. The speaker tells us how she tries to 'handle and hold', 'mind and attend', 'bind' and 'feel the hurt'. She operates with great tenderness, seen especially in her delicate descriptions of her partner's collar-bone and lungs as fragile 'porcelain' and fine 'silk' respectively. Though with its emphasis on touch, the language conveys a sense of physical, loving intimacy, at the same time there is a sense of a distance, of an inner core that is difficult to reach.

Repetition of the phrase 'only then' is significant. Appearing five times in the poem, mostly at the starts of lines, it conveys the tense delicacy of the operation. At each stage of slowly increasing intimacy the speaker has to wait until it is safe, as if for permission, before she can move onwards and inwards. As if, at any stage, or at any false move, the alarm bells of his defences might go off and she might be prevented from going any further. Or even worse might happen. It is like she is moving through a series of locked doors, or over a booby-trapped landscape or creeping past watchtowers. Each time she has to unlock the door through touch, defuse the potential explosive through love and then take the next careful step on her journey. Commas at the ends of these lines add to the sense of the pauses taken before the speaker moves forwards. 'Hypervigilance' is another form of PTSD in which the sufferer develops an extreme and obsessive sensitivity to possible threats. The sufferer cannot relax; they are constantly on guard. Touching her partner's body, the speaker must be incredibly careful not to be perceived as a potential threat.

The access she is allowed increases as the poem progresses. At first, for instance, the phrase 'only then' is succeeded by 'would he let me', highlighting the need for his permission before she can continue. The three similarly structured stanzas, numbers 4,5 and 6, all beginning the simplest conjunction 'and', suggest that, essentially, in each of these the speaker is doing variations of the same thing, tracing his wounds. But that repetition allows the soldier to get used to the tactile intimacy, perhaps even to drop his guard a bit, perhaps even relax a little, so that by the seventh couplet there is progress. From here on in all the remaining 'only thens' are succeeded by her actions – 'could I', 'did I'.

The poem's form contributes to the sense of tentative development. Irregular, unmetred, it is impossible to predict the length of the lines in each couplet. Hence the form of the poem is akin to the speaker feeling her way, working out what to do as she goes along. Or we could relate the form to the soldier. Judged from the outside he might appear fine. But that outer order would only hide the disorder within. But this inner uncertainty, hers, his or both, is contained within the consistent use of the couplet form. At no time does this form break down. It holds and it endures. The use of rhyme also holds out the possibility of harmony, as rhyme is a form of sonic resolution, of words fitting together musically. It's significant, then, that not all the couplets rhyme and the overall pattern of the poem is towards looser rhymes. Compare, for example, the opening rhymes, 'phase/ days' and 'trace/ face' with the end words in the last two couplets, 'mine/ which' and 'closed/ close'. Read pessimistically, this loosening could suggest that actually the couple are not, in fact, getting closer together as the poem develops. Read optimistically, the loosening of a tight rhyme pattern might suggest the easing of tension.

Simon Armitage himself has suggested that a helpful way in to analysing a poem is to pick about five words that interest you as a reader and to put these words under the microscope. There's a word in this poem that immediately leaps out at me. It leaps out because it seems incongruous, completely out of place in this context. That word is 'foetus'. Describing the fragment of a bullet buried in the man's chest as a 'foetus' is an extraordinary thing to do. Why? Because normally we associate seeing a foetus within a body with women, with pregnancy and with childbirth. When parents-to-be first see the image of their foetus this is normally an incredibly happy and humbling moment in their lives. A foetus = new life, new beginnings, new hope for the future. In this man's chest the image is unnatural and almost monstrous. Bringing the reader up short, it very powerfully conveys the idea that his damage is growing within him and at some point will fully develop and be released.

Enduring love

Noticeably Armitage chose some very similar words close together at the end of the poem. Normally such repetition is frowned upon in prose narrative, especially when it could easily have been avoided through the use of synonyms. For example, the poet could easily have referred to the 'mine' as being buried deep in the soldier's 'head' or 'brain' or 'thoughts'. But, instead he chose 'mind'. Similarly, in the penultimate and final line he could have used 'shut', instead of 'closed', or 'near', instead of 'close'.

So, why didn't he avoid this clumsiness? What does he gain? The sonic closeness between 'mine' and 'mind' signals that the former has nearly filled up the latter. The soldier's mind has almost become a mine. This connection is cemented using the adjective 'sweating'. Applied to and personifying the inanimate 'mine', it collapses the distinction between it and the soldier. In a profound way, the soldier himself has become 'a sweating, unexploded mine' that could go off at any time. Armitage's poem ends with the speaker note quite having reached the heart of the trauma. As she gets closest to the 'source' the soldier tenses up again: 'every nerve in his body had tightened'. The doors she had opened in him are now suddenly 'closed'. In this context, her coming 'close' could imply that she failed, she missed. However, the use of almost an identical word as first a verb and then an adjective to describe first his action and then hers, suggests another more optimistic reading. The sharing of this final word is like the consistent use of the couplet form. It implies shared experience, a mutuality that will endure.

The Manhunt crunched:

FIRST – INTIMATE – ONLY – FROZEN – EXPLORE – BLOWN – HOLD – DAMAGED – MIND – RUDDER – FINGER – SILK – BIND – BROKEN – FEEL – GRAZED – SKIRTING – THEN – FOETUS – BULLET – SEARCH – MINE – DEEP – CLOSED – CLOSE

Nettles and *The Manhunt* both deal with the after effects of soldiers' experience of warfare and, in particular, the long-lasting psychological effects. Both poems explore this topic through the experience of individuals. Though on the surface, Scannell's narrator seems to have coped better, re-establishing a normal family life, just underneath this surface lies a violent rage. Like Armitage's soldier, the trauma is buried and like Armitage's soldier its release is fraught with peril. But, at least Scannell's narrator is able to tell his own experience - a stark comparison with the soldier's ominous silence in *The Manhunt.*

Ingrid De Kok, *My Father Would Not Show Us*

Scaling history down to the personal

The most striking line in De Kok's elegy for her dead father is line 24: 'Everything he hears is white'. With the synesthesia converting sound into sight and the complex implications of describing all sounds universally as the same, 'white', it would be a striking line in any poem. But in a poem by a South African writer, especially one like De Kok who grew up during Apartheid, it carries greater significance and resonance. In this context only hearing whiteness might signal deafness and blindness to the experiences of black people. There are two ways of interpreting the poem in this light. Firstly that the way the father behaves within his family is an analogy on a domestic scale to how other people have refused to engage with the realities of South African society on a historical and political level. Or, the father's refusal to engage, his turning away indicates his own refusal or inability to face this reality. Perhaps, however, the best way of understanding the poem is as expressing both of the above. In other words, that how the father behaves within the home reflects his lack of interaction with the wider social reality.

He walked away

Certainly, the key characteristics of the father seem to be his turning away and <u>not</u> showing his children life's harsher realities. After death, his face has been 'organised for me to see', a strange choice of verb which suggests that things have been deliberately arranged to create a specific impression. And the passive construction 'is organised' means we are not told who does this organising or for what reason. Immediately we are alerted to the idea of things being arranged to create particular impressions.

When the poet remembers their father from their childhood they recall a 'wry smile', an adjective that suggests some sort of secret amusement, and his face is described as 'half-turned', equally towards and away from her. In addition, the father, we are told, characteristically 'hid' from something. The importance of what appears to have become a strategy or habit of avoidance is emphasised through immediate repetition of the verb; 'he hid away'. The following phrase, 'behind the curtains' implies he put a barrier up between

 himself and his children, but also between his home, his life and the wider world beyond. Later he is described as being 'under the counterpane' in bed. There he upholds another distance by not speaking. Furthermore, he is also described as staying 'inside' and as passive - 'he lay' is repeated three times and forms the final image of the father. Inside, under,

behind all signal the father's difficulty with, or refusal to engage with his children. As within the home, so within society. By extension this avoidance suggests lack of engagement with the complex, often violent and fundamentally unjust political reality outside in South African society. The line 'he turned, he turned away' suggests the father did not face his responsibilities within the family. We can determine that his behaviour parallels failures to engage with the reality of SA society and, specifically the injustice of Apartheid. In this way, De Klok's poem evokes Edmund Burke's famous observation that 'all it takes for evil to succeed is for good to do nothing'.

As significant as this avoidance and distancing strategy is the fact that the father 'would not show' his children something. Obviously, this is the title of the poem and its importance is signaled by being repeated three times in the poem [though the final time 'would' changes to 'could']. While this could be read as paternal and protective behaviour, in some ways this not showing is perhaps worse than his own avoidance of reality. In South Africa it  could, indeed, be read as a deliberate attempt to hide the truth and to keep his children ignorant. At first we do not know what he refuses to show. Only in fifth stanza does the poet become more explicit; he could not show them 'how to die'. What might she mean by this? There are at least three possible interpretations. Firstly, it could mean that the father refuses to show the children, as in he could not bring himself to. If, however, we read the verb as being in the future tense, it could mean that when he died he did not show them how to do this properly. Thirdly, whereas 'would' implies a deliberate act of will, 'could' suggests the father might not have been able to do this. However we read it, the line raises fundamental questions about how we should manage our deaths and by implication how we should lead our lives. The implication appears to be that the father wasn't able to provide the example his children needed. In this way, the poem could be read as a kind of anti-elegy, criticising rather than mourning the dead.

Not turning away

Perhaps this is why the speaker would have liked her childhood to be a 'louder, braver place'. Perhaps the reference to a 'crowded' house with a 'tin roof' reveals that she thinks of these louder, braver places as being the sorts of houses typically lived in by South Africa's black population. De Kok has written about her country's Truth and Reconciliation commission, which dealt with the aftermath of decades of Apartheid. According to Wikipedia, she also runs 'various capacity building, civic and trade union programmes' for her community. She, certainly, has not looked away, not turned her face, like her father, 'to the wall' and remained passive. Instead she actively engages with her society and deals with its tortured, racist past. And the poet does not shy away from facing her uncommunicative father either. Her poem does not avoid reality, or organise this material to make a more sympathetic or favourable impression. Nor does she massage the past to hide or excuse its ugliness. Instead her poem faces the harsh truths about her father with honesty and integrity.

My Father Would Not Show Us is a free verse poem. There is no metre, rhyme scheme or set stanza form. With stanzas of three, four, five and six lines, and lines varying from three to nine words long, the poem is highly irregular and its form is constantly changing. On the one hand, this could indicate the lack of an example that was set for the poet to follow. Her father failed to provide her with a pattern or order by which to live life bravely. Hence the poet has to find her own way, forge her own course, as best she can. But on the other hand, flip this around, and the irregular free verse form shows she is liberated from any pre-set pattern. She doesn't have to follow her father's footsteps, she doesn't have to repeat her father's  or anyone else's example. She can, and does, forge her own path and create an example that others, as loud and as brave her, may follow.

My Father Would Not Show Us crunched:

FATHER'S – DEAD – ORGANISED – COLD – UNNATURALLY – YET – INVERTED – SOFT – FROZEN – ALLOWED – MIGHT – BRAVER – TIN – HAILED – HALF-TURNED – DIE – HID – BEHIND – CURLING – INSIDE – RECALL – MORNING – DOGS – WHITE – NOT – AWAY – UNDER – WORD - WALL

'The best love poems are known / as such to the lovers
alone.'

LES MURRAY

Comparing the poems

In the exam you will have to complete two poetry tasks, both comparative in nature. In the first you'll be asked to compare a specific poem printed on the paper with any one from the anthology of your choice. In the second task you're required to compare two unseen poems. For the first question you have 35 minutes, for the second you've 45 minutes. No doubt it will have struck you that 35 minutes is not a lot of time to write a decent comparative essay. What you certainly cannot afford to do is dilly dally over the choice of the second poem. In your thorough preparation for this exam you should already have matched up all the poems in several different possible combinations, so that as soon as you see the printed poem you already know with which poem you're going to compare it. Not only that, but you should also have worked out the key points of comparison and contrast.

According to Edexcel, 'responses that are considerably unbalanced' will not reach the top grades, so you can't write predominantly on one of the poems. The examiners are also looking for 'perceptive comparison' on a range of 'similarities and differences'. Significantly, for a top grade as well as evaluating the poets' use of language, showing an excellent understanding of context and employing precise terminology, you have to develop a 'perceptive grasp of form and structure'. Often this is the most challenging aspect of poetry for pupils and, hence, it's an aspect we've covered in detail in each of our essays.

The best way to develop an overview of the relationships between these poems is to write down all the titles on a large piece of paper. First, map out what the poems have in common and after how they are different to each other. It's very useful to have one piece of paper that captures these textual relationships. Use colour, icons, venn diagrams, anything that helps make the connections memorable. Another useful exercise that can be done time and again in the run up to the exam is to write the titles of all the poems on paper, cut these out individually, turn them over and then pick up three pieces of paper randomly. The task then is to say how two of the poems are similar and how the third is different. Do this quickly, a couple of minutes or so, in order that you focus on key aspects. Put the titles back in the mix, pick three more at random and repeat the exercise, over and over again.

Clearly there is a myriad of possible comparisons and the following is by no means a comprehensive list. Nor are our suggestions ones you should slavishly follow, obviously. But, hopefully, the following will provide a starting point, a launchpad for your own thinking.

La Belle Dame could be compared to *She Walks in Beauty* as both poems feature an echanting female and an enchanted male. Like the one in *My Last Duchess*, the relationship in Keats's poem is destructive, though in Browning's poem the female character is the victim. *La Belle Dame* shares with *Neutral Tones* a sense of desolation, in part projected onto a landscape. Keats's poem could be contrasted with the far more idealistic, innocent presentation of love in *Sonnet 43* and Baillie's poem, or, at a push, the much more light-hearted description of potential lovers in *1st Date*.

Family relationships are the heart of **A Child to His Sick Grandfather**, linking it to *My Father Would Not Show Us* and *Nettles*. In terms of its plain style Baillie's poem could be compared to Wordsworth's and Barrett-Browning's. The pure, compassionate love the child expresses links it to

Sonnet 43 and could be contrasted with darker depictions of love in many other of the poems, including Duffy's *Valentine*.

Wordsworth's **A Complaint** is about the break-up of a relationship, as is Hardy's *Neutral Tones*. In Jennings's poem *One Flesh* the relationship endures, despite the separation that has grown between the wife and her husband. In this respect, all of these poems could be compared to *The Manhunt*. A marrirage gone horribly wrong is one way to describe *My Last Duchess*.

Browning's poem is also a dramatic monologue, which connects it to *1st Date*, *A Child to His Sick Grandfather*, *The Manhunt* and, possibly, *Love's Dog* which could be interpreted to be written in the voice of a dog! *1st Date* and *I wanna be yours* are also light, comic poems that use everyday bits and bobs from pop culture and a modern idiom. The narrator's ardent amour in the latter could also connect it to Byron's poem.

A small group of poems set the relationships between characters within a wider frame of relationships between individuals and society. Both *Nettles* and *The Manhunt* feature characters haunted by their experience of warfare and in whom shadows from the past continue to smother the present. Though De Kok's poem can be read as being about entirely about family tensions, the fact that the poem is about avoidance and was written in South Africa suggests that the father's uncommunicative and evasive behaviour embodies a wider reluctance to engage with that country's turbulent recent history.

Terminology task

The following is a list of poetry terminology and short definitions of the terms. Unfortunately, cruel, malicious individuals (i.e. us) have scrambled them up. Your task is to unscramble the list, matching each term to the correct definition. Good luck!

Term	Definition
Imagery	Vowel rhyme, e.g. 'bat' and 'lag'
Metre	An implicit comparison in which one thing is said to be another
Rhythm	Description in poetry
Simile	A conventional metaphor, such as a 'dove' for peace
Metaphor	A metrical foot comprising an unstressed followed by a stressed beat
Symbol	
Iambic	A line with five beats
Pentameter	Description in poetry using metaphor, simile or personification
Enjambment	A repeated pattern of ordered sound
Caesura	An explicit comparison of two things, using 'like' or 'as'
Dramatic monologue	Words, or combinations of words, whose sounds mimic their meaning
Figurative imagery	
Onomatopoeia	Words in a line starting with the same letter or sound
Lyric	A strong break in a line, usually signalled by punctuation
Adjective	A regular pattern of beats in each line
Alliteration	A narrative poem with an alternating four and three beat line
Ballad	A word that describes a noun
Sonnet	A 14-line poem following several possible rhyme schemes
Assonance	When a sentence steps over the end of a line and continues into the next line or stanza
Sensory imagery	
Quatrain	Description that uses the senses
Diction	A four-line stanza
Personification	Inanimate objects given human characteristics
	A poem written in the voice of a character
	A poem written in the first person, focusing on the emotional experience of the narrator
	A term to describe the vocabulary used in a poem.

A sonnet of revision activities

1. Reverse millionaire: 10,000 points if students can guess the poem just from one word from it. You can vary the difficulty as much as you like. For example, 'clams', would be fairly easily identifiable as from Sexton's poem whereas 'fleet' would be more difficult. 1000 points if students can name the poem from a single phrase or image – 'portion out the stars and dates'. 100 points for a single line. 10 points for recognising the poem from a stanza. Play individually or in teams.

2. Research the poet. Find one sentence about them that you think sheds light on their poem in the anthology. Compare with your classmates. Or find a couple more lines or a stanza by a poet and see if others can recognise the writer from their lines.

3. Write a cento based on one or more of the poems. A cento is a poem constructed from lines from other poems. Difficult, creative, but also fun, perhaps.

4. Read 3 or 4 other poems by one of the poets. Write a pastiche. See if classmates can recognise the poet you're imitating.

5. Write the introduction for a critical guide on the poems aimed at next year's yr. 10 class.

6. Use the poet Glynn Maxwell's typology of poems to arrange the poems into different groups. In his excellent book, *On Poetry*, Maxwell suggests poems have four dominant aspects, which he calls solar,

lunar, musical and visual. A solar poem hits home, is immediately striking. A lunar poem, by contrast, is more mysterious and might not give up its meanings so easily. Ideally a lunar poem will haunt your imagination. Written mainly for the ear, a musical poem focuses on the sounds of language, rather than the meanings. Think of Lewis Carroll's *Jabberwocky*. A visual poem is self-conscious about how it looks to the eye. Concrete poems are the ultimate visual poems. According to Maxwell, the very best poems are strong in each dimension. Try applying this test to each poem. Which ones come out on top?

7. Maxwell also recommends conceptualising the context in which the words of the poem are created or spoken. Which poems would suit being read around a camp fire? Which would be better declaimed from the top of a tall building? Which might you imagine on a stage? Which ones are more like conversation overheard? Which are the easiest and which the most difficult to place?

8. Mr Maxwell is a fund of interesting ideas. He suggests all poems dramatise a battle between the forces of whiteness and blackness, nothingness and somethingness, sound and silence, life and death. In each poem, what is the dynamic between whiteness and blackness? Which appears to have the upper hand?

9. Still thinking in terms of evaluation, consider the winnowing effect of time. Which of the modern poems do you think might be still read in 20, a 100 or 200 years? Why?

10. Give yourself only the first and last line of one of the poems. Without

peeking at the original, try to fill in the middle. Easy level: write in prose. Expert level: attempt verse.

11. According to Russian Formalist critics, poetry performs a 'controlled explosion on ordinary language'. What evidence can you find in this selection of controlled linguistic detonations?

12. A famous musician once said that though he wasn't the best at playing all the notes, nobody played the silences better. In Japanese garden water features the sound of a water drop is designed to make us notice the silence around it. Try reading one of the poems in the light of these comments, focusing on the use of white space, caesuras, punctuation – all the devices that create the silence on which the noise of the poem rests.

13. In *Notes on the Art of Poetry*, Dylan Thomas wrote that 'the best craftsmanship always leaves holes and gaps in the works of the poem so that something that is not in the poem can creep, crawl, flash or thunder in'. Examine a poem in the light of this comment, looking for its holes and gaps. If you discover these, what 'creeps', 'crawls' or 'flashes' in to fill them?

14. Different types of poems conceive the purpose of poetry differently. Broadly speaking Augustan poets of the eighteenth century aimed to impress their readers with the wit of their ideas and the elegance of the expression. In contrast, Romantic poets wished to move their readers' hearts. Characteristically Victorian poets aimed to teach the readers some kind of moral principle or example. Self-involved, avant-

garde Modernists weren't overly bothered about finding, never mind pleasing, a general audience. What impact do the Edexcel anthology poems seek? Do they seek to amuse, appeal to the heart, teach us something? Are they like soliloquies – the overheard inner workings of thinking – or more like speeches or mini-plays? Try placing each poem somewhere on the following continuums. Then create a few continuums of your own. As ever, comparison with your classmates will prove illuminating.

Emotional...intellectual

Feelings...ideas

Internal...external

Contemplative...rhetorical

Open...guarded

GLOSSARY

ALLITERATION – the repetition of consonants at the start of neighbouring words in a line

ANAPAEST - a three beat pattern of syllables, unstress, unstress, stress. E.g. 'on the moon', 'to the coast', 'anapaest'

ANTITHESIS - the use of balanced opposites

APOSTROPHE – a figure of speech addressing a person, object or idea

ASSONANCE – vowel rhyme, e.g. sod and block

BLANK VERSE – unrhymed lines of iambic pentameter

BLAZON – a male lover describing the parts of his beloved

CADENCE – the rise of fall of sounds in a line of poetry

CAESURA – a distinct break in a poetic line, usually marked by punctuation

COMPLAINT – a type of love poem concerned with loss and mourning

CONCEIT – an extended metaphor

CONSONANCE – rhyme based on consonants only, e.g. book and back

COUPLET – a two-line stanza, conventionally rhyming

DACTYL – the reverse pattern to the anapaest; stress, unstress, unstress. E.g. 'Strong as a'

DRAMATIC MONOLOGUE – a poem written in the voice of a distinct character

ELEGY – a poem in mourning for someone dead

END-RHYME – rhyming words at the end of a line

END-STOPPED – the opposite of enjambment; i.e. when the sentence and the poetic line stop at the same point

ENJAMBMENT – where sentences run over the end of lines and stanzas

FIGURATIVE LANGUAGE – language that is not literal, but employs figures of speech, such as metaphor, simile and personification

FEMININE RHYME – a rhyme that ends with an unstressed syllable or unstressed syllables.

FREE VERSE – poetry without metre or a regular, set form

GOTHIC – a style of literature characterised by psychological horror, dark deeds and uncanny events

HEROIC COUPLETS – pairs of rhymed lines in iambic pentameter

HYPERBOLE – extreme exaggeration

IAMBIC – a metrical pattern of a weak followed by a strong stress, ti-TUM, like a heart beat

IMAGERY – the umbrella term for description in poetry. Sensory imagery refers to descriptions that appeal to sight, sound and so forth; figurative imagery refers to the use of devices such as metaphor, simile and personification

JUXTAPOSITION – two things placed together to create a strong contrast

LYRIC – an emotional, personal poem usually with a first-person speaker

MASCULINE RHYME – an end rhyme on a strong syllable

METAPHOR – an implicit comparison in which one thing is said to be another

METAPHYSICAL – a type of poetry characterised by wit and extended metaphors

METRE – the regular pattern organising sound and rhythm in a poem

MOTIF – a repeated image or pattern of language, often carrying thematic significance

OCTET OR OCTAVE – the opening eight lines of a sonnet

ONOMATOPOEIA – bang, crash, wallop

PENTAMETER – a poetic line consisting of five beats

PERSONIFICATION – giving human characteristics to inanimate things

PLOSIVE – a type of alliteration using 'p' and 'b' sounds

QUATRAIN – a four-line stanza

REFRAIN – a line or lines repeated like a chorus

ROMANTIC – A type of poetry characterised by a love of nature, by strong emotion and heightened tone

SESTET – the last six lines in a sonnet

SIMILE – an explicit comparison of two different things

SONNET – a form of poetry with fourteen lines and a variety of possible set rhyme patterns

SPONDEE – two strong stresses together in a line of poetry

STANZA – the technical name for a verse

SYMBOL – something that stands in for something else. Often a concrete representation of an idea.

SYNTAX – the word order in a sentence. doesn't Without sense English syntax make. Syntax is crucial to sense: For example, though it uses all the same words, 'the man eats the fish' is not the same as 'the fish eats the man'

TERCET – a three-line stanza

TETRAMETER – a line of poetry consisting of four beats

TROCHEE – the opposite of an iamb; stress, unstress, strong, weak.

VILLANELLE – a complex interlocking verse form in which lines are recycled

VOLTA – the 'turn' in a sonnet from the octave to the sestet

Recommended reading

Atherton, C. & Green, A. Teaching English Literature 16-19. NATE, 2013

Bate, J. Ted Hughes, The Unauthorised Life. William Collins, 2016

Bowen et al. The Art of Poetry, vol.1-4. Peripeteia Press, 2015-16

Brinton, I. Contemporary Poetry. CUP, 2009

Eagleton, T. How to Read a Poem. Wiley & Sons, 2006

Fry, S. The Ode Less Travelled. Arrow, 2007

Hamilton, I. & Noel-Todd, J. Oxford Companion to Modern Poetry, OUP, 2014

Heaney, S. The Government of the Tongue. Farrar, Straus & Giroux, 1976

Herbert, W. & Hollis, M. Strong Words. Bloodaxe, 2000

Howarth, P. The Cambridge Introduction to Modernist Poetry. CUP, 2012

Hurley, M. & O'Neill, M. Poetic Form, An Introduction. CUP, 2012

Meally, M. & Bowen, N. The Art of Writing English Literature Essays, Peripeteia Press, 2014

Maxwell, G. On Poetry. Oberon Masters, 2012

Padel, R. 52 Ways of Looking at a Poem. Vintage, 2004

Padel, R. The Poem and the Journey. Vintage, 2008

Paulin, T. The Secret Life of Poems. Faber & Faber, 2011

Schmidt, M. Lives of the Poets, Orion, 1998

Wolosky, S. The Art of Poetry: How to Read a Poem. OUP, 2008.

About the author

Head of English and freelance writer, Neil Bowen has a Masters Degree in Literature & Education from Cambridge University and is a member of Ofqual's experts panel for English. He is the author of *The Art of Writing English Essays for GCSE*, co-author of *The Art of Writing English Essays for A-level and Beyond* and of *The Art of Poetry*, volumes 1-10. Neil runs the peripeteia project, bridging the gap between A-level and degree level English courses: www.peripeteia.webs.com.

Valentine #2

Not a spray of roses or box of chocs.
I give you a pair of my old pants.
Though they are only one
They are also a pair.
(Like us).

Here, have them.

They might blind you with tears –
Like boxers,
Only they're actually y-fronts –
(Cotton, Marks & Sparks)

Not a hotel in Paris or candlelit dinner.
I give you my old pants.
You look like you're crying.

Take them. Please.
They've holes in some inconvenient places.
I am trying to tell the truth.

Though their elastic's gone,
If you pull them apart
Hard enough
The will ping back together.

A bit like us,
hopefully.

Printed in Great Britain
by Amazon